Saved from Hell:
one woman's real life account

Lori Haider

Saved from **HELL**
one woman's real life account

Unless otherwise noted all scripture quotations are taken from the *King James Version* of the Bible. Public domain.

Scripture quotations marked amp are taken from *The Amplified Bible*. New Testament copyright © 1958, 1987 by The Lockman Foundation, La Habra, California. Used by permission.

Scripture taken from the *Holy Bible, New International Version*®. Copyright © 1973, 1978, 1984 Biblica. Used by permission of Zondervan. All rights reserved.

The "NIV" and "New International Version" trademarks are registered in the United States Patent and Trademark Office by Biblica. Use of either trademark requires the permission of Biblica.

Scripture taken from *The Message*. Copyright © 1993, 1994, 1995, 1996, 2000, 2001, 2002. Used by permission of NavPress Publishing Group.

Scripture quotations marked NLT are taken from the *Holy Bible, New Living Translation,* copyright 1996, 2004. Used by permission of Tyndale House Publishers, Inc., Wheaton, Illinois 60189. All rights reserved.

Saved from HELL: *one woman's real life account*

30 29 28 27 26 25   10 09 08 07 06 05

ISBN 13: 978-0-9815379-9-3
ISBN 10: 0-9815379-9-5

Copyright © 2010 by Lori Haider

Printed in the United States of America. All rights reserved under International Copyright Law. Contents and/or cover may not be reproduced in whole or in part in any form without the express written consent of the Publisher.

Table of Contents

Foreword ix

My Story

Chapter 1	How It All Began 1
Chapter 2	Lured Into New Age 5
Chapter 3	Becoming a Psychic 11
Chapter 4	One Wrong Turn After Another 21
Chapter 5	Planning My Suicide 29
Chapter 6	Seeing Into the Spirit Realm 37
Chapter 7	My Prison Cell in Hell 49

New Age

Chapter 8	Comparing New Age and Bible Doctrine 65
Chapter 9	Searching for God 77

Satan and Demons

Chapter 10	Liberty to the Captives 87
Chapter 11	How Demons Torment People 93
Chapter 12	Casting Out Devils 101
Chapter 13	A Christian's Authority 107
Chapter 14	My Deliverance Process 111
Chapter 15	Setting People Free 117

Hell

Chapter 16	Hell Is Real 127
Chapter 17	Life in Hell 133
Chapter 18	Are You Saved? 139

*Behold, the Lord's hand
is not shortened,
that it cannot save;
neither His ear heavy,
that it cannot hear.*
—Isaiah 59:1

Foreword

> *"You know that I have not hesitated to preach anything that would be helpful to you . . . I have declared to . . . turn to God in repentance and have faith in our Lord Jesus . . . [I am] compelled by the Spirit . . . not knowing what will happen to me . . . I consider my life worth nothing to me, if only I may finish the race and complete the task the Lord Jesus has given me—the task of testifying to the gospel of God's grace."*
>
> —Acts 20:20–24 (NIV)

This scripture, spoken by the Apostle Paul, embodies the message of *Saved From Hell*. Verse 20 in the New King James Version says, "I kept back nothing. . . ." And that is how I have written this book. After what I have experienced, my single desire is to warn people about hell and tell them about the wonderful life available through Jesus Christ. By sharing what I have learned and showing you what I have seen, you will experience the same extreme alarm God gave me. And my prayer is that you will never experience the horrors of hell.

In this book, I wrote openly about my own life, in order for God to speak to you about your life, as you read it. As I wrestled with the Lord about being so transparent, He spoke to my heart saying, "This is what it took for you to be saved. Please tell others, so they can be saved as well."

This book is an expression of Jude 1:22–23 (NKJV), which says, "*. . . on some have compassion . . . but others save with fear, pulling them out of the fire. . . .*" My story reveals the patient mercy of God and the coming judgment for those who ultimately refuse Christ.

I've waited years, since my dramatic conversion in 2002, before writing this book. These years were filled with a time of intense preparation, which included attending two Bible schools and serving in supportive ministry in my home church (in street evangelism, prayer and worship). God used this time to carve character into my heart and mature me as a Christian.

Most importantly, He spent these years teaching me how much He loved me. Early after my salvation, I tried to write this book, unknowingly propelled by fear and guilt. However, the Lord stopped me. Concerned I was displeasing Him, I prayed, seeking direction. He spoke plainly in my heart, with the tone of a protective father, saying, "I don't *ever* want you to speak of these things until you know how much I love you." I was stunned. He further explained that I was His daughter and He saved me because He deeply loved me. He went on saying that He didn't save me so I could work for Him or be some spectacle to people. Now, after a process of being restored by His love, He's released me to share this message, so you can read it as a message of His same, deep love for you.

I would like to thank each person who trained and mentored me. There are simply too many names to list, but I am grateful to each of you. Most of all, I thank and honor my parents for their unselfish kindness to me throughout my life and for their courage in supporting me to complete the challenging assignment I've been given.

As you read the pages of this book, I pray you will understand the great price Jesus paid in offering His life as a sacrifice so you and I could be saved from hell. My hope is that this book compels you to be saved if you are not. And if you are saved, I trust that you will be inspired to tell everyone you can how they, too, can be saved.

Lori Haider

My Story

Chapter 1

How it All Began

I grew up in a loving home and had a good, stable upbringing. We were a farm family and lived in a small town in the Midwest. Life was simple. All of my parent's five children were honor roll students. Our family never missed a church service on Sunday. No one in my family was alcoholic and no one used drugs. Our family was free from divorce. My parents didn't even have financial problems.

My parents always sought to do the right thing and be a good neighbor. They often helped others in need, never asking for something in return. They cared for their elderly parents and gave their lives to their children. My parents even did without vacations to provide for their children's school clothes and college educations. Every birthday was complete with a homemade cake. Every Christmas had many family gatherings, food and presents. And, I remember many happy evenings playing board games around our large kitchen table. By all accounts, I was blessed by heaven with the best family life could offer.

Harassed Since Childhood

However, I had spiritual struggles during my upbringing that my family didn't understand. As a young child, I often felt a darkness settle on me. And when the darkness came, I didn't have any control over it. But worse, I didn't know where to go for help. Although I won't go into detail, when I was at the age of five I was molested. I am only sharing this information so you will understand that this was a way for demons to gain entrance into my life. I want to make it very clear that the molester was not a member of my family, and my parents never knew anything about it. Had they known, they would have done everything in their power to have protected me.

One night when I was nine years old, I awoke from a restless sleep only to see an evil spirit staring at me. I was just a young, innocent child and had no idea that it was a demon. To me, it was a "creature." The creature was much larger than me and screeched when it realized that I saw it. It then reached toward me with its hand, which was both a hand and a claw, and scratched me. However, when it scratched me, it was able to reach through my body and scratch my spirit.

This large creature was joined by other creatures and I watched them torment my family. I was so scared. I didn't really know what they were doing. As a child, I only knew they made my family very sad. I was terrified and didn't know how to stop these ugly, evil looking creatures. For years, I cried before going to sleep every night. I would try to stay awake as long as I could. Eventually, when I would fall asleep, I often had bad dreams. And the bad dreams never stopped. They continued throughout my childhood, teenage, and young adult life. It was only after I became born again that the tormenting dreams ended.

Although I never saw the creatures after that first encounter, I could feel them around me. Sometimes I physically felt them striking me. It was after I was "scratched" by the creature that I began thinking about taking my life.

By the time I turned 12 years old, I was exhausted from the struggle. I remember seeing and feeling something very large and dark trying to enter my body. I tried to physically fight it off for days, but it was much stronger than I was. And when I stopped resisting it, I could feel it come into my body, and there was nothing I could do about it. I felt as though this "thing" was molesting me on the inside. I felt completely violated. Even after it was inside of me, I tried to fight against it. But it was already in me, and I knew it. I cried and cried. I was so afraid and felt as though my body had become a prison I had to live in.

I tried to tell my mom what happened but I didn't know how to describe it. She tried to help me, but she could only deal with my "symptoms" from a physical and mental side. She didn't know I was in a spiritual battle.

I grew up in a very religious home. Although we regularly attended church, we didn't know how to have a personal relationship with Jesus Christ. The church we attended didn't preach about how to be saved. But it did preach that heaven and hell were real and that Jesus was God's son. Even if my family understood that I was in a spiritual battle, they wouldn't have known what to do about it.

Strange Illnesses

I began suffering from a lot of sicknesses. Once, I became very physically weak and felt as though all of the strength had left my body. In fact, I stopped walking for several months and stayed home from school a lot. My parents were very concerned and took me to many doctors. After being tested for many things, the doctors told my parents there was nothing physically wrong with me and that I would just have to walk. I remembered leaving the hospital thinking, *Oh God, I'm going to have to live this way for the rest of my life.* From then on, I periodically felt as though something was holding me down. I didn't know how to explain to my parents what was happening to me. Over the course of time, I just learned to live with the darkness.

Suicidal Thoughts as a Teen

When I was about 12, my cousin committed suicide on my parent's property. His death affected me a lot—mainly because I was also contemplating suicide at the same time. The suicidal thoughts continued throughout my teenage years. I really didn't want to die, but intense feelings of sorrow and depression would come on me, and I felt as though I couldn't push the darkness away. When that happened, suicide seemed like the only way out. I didn't know anything about demons as a child and teenager. I only knew that something was very wrong, and I didn't know where to go for help. I tried to "fix" my inner torment in any way I could think of. I began "purging" myself after eating, and suffered with bulimia for many years. However, bulimia for me was not so much about food. It was my attempt to get rid of the darkness that I felt inside of me. I remember one time when I was throwing up, I prayed to God to please help me purge this awful thing.

Nothing Changed as I Grew Older

I had hoped that as I grew into adulthood, I would outgrow this torment and that the darkness that clung to me would somehow drop off. But that never happened. Instead, things got worse. I constantly had battles in my mind and body. Devils don't just go away. They remain with you for life if they are not cast out in the name of Jesus.

During college, I sought and received treatment for bulimia. While going through the twelve-step treatment program, a Christian pastor came in for one session to discuss believing in a higher power. In this step of the program, we had to choose to turn our lives over to the care of God, *as we understood Him*. I listened as the pastor spoke. In my heart, I could tell he had something that I didn't have. I didn't know what it was, but I wanted it. He told us that his higher power was Jesus, but because of the organization's policies, he was required to say *Higher Power*. This way, each person could *choose* the power of their understanding.

After his session, I was confused and frustrated. I believed in Jesus, but I didn't have what he had. And I couldn't find out how to get what he had because he couldn't talk about it! I kept replaying in my mind what the pastor had said. I finally concluded that Christianity apparently didn't work for me, since I didn't have what he had.

When the twelve-step program was over, I began seeing a counselor who diagnosed me with mild, recurrent depression, prescribed antidepressants, and told me that I could get better with "talk therapy." (Please note: Some people require medication for depression. *DO NOT* stop taking your medication if needed. My problem was a spiritual problem. When I took medication, it didn't have any effect on me.)

I was in therapy for a year and didn't have any good results. The sadness never got better. In fact, just the opposite happened; my depression grew worse. I finally came to the conclusion that I would have to live this way.

After college, I began working in the corporate world. By then, I learned to hide my sadness in public. On the outside, my life appeared to be very normal. No one would have guessed how much inner torment I battled every day.

Chapter 2

LURED INTO NEW AGE

My first encounter with New Age occurred when I was 26 years old. I had graduated from college several years earlier and had a rewarding job in video production. My career had an exciting future. I travelled a lot and even met a few celebrities. I had a great boyfriend. We talked about getting married and decided to live together. This was what all of my friends did, so I figured it would be okay, even though I knew my parents weren't crazy about it. Life seemed to be taking off for me. From all outward appearances, my future appeared promising. However, I continued to carry an emptiness inside of me that wouldn't go away. Although I was surrounded by many friends, I always felt alone.

One evening after I got home from work, I decided to relax in our living room. A TV program came on that grabbed my attention. It touched my heart because it spoke to the emptiness I was feeling. The program appeared to be a news documentary. The host was interviewing guests who shared about their experiences with the supernatural. They discussed how the spirit realm was real and how angels could help you connect to the spirit realm.

At this point in my life, I had stopped thinking about God. I assumed I was going to heaven because I had never killed anyone or stolen a car. But beyond that, I didn't think much of God, heaven, or hell. I didn't know if heaven and hell were real places. The host and guests on this program openly discussed how they found meaning and direction in life through experiences they had with the spirit realm. I was immediately drawn in and began thinking that maybe I could fill the emptiness I felt through contacting the "spirit realm" and "God."

The people on the program shared how a family member or spouse had died. Pictures of their loved ones appeared on the screen as they talked about the anguish they experienced after the death of their loved one. They told how they were able to find closure and direction for their lives after contacting their deceased loved ones.[1]

I thought of my oldest sister who had died several years earlier. Her life was cut short when she died in a plane crash at the age of 24. She was away at college. And the day before she was supposed to fly home for Thanksgiving, a friend invited her to go on a plane ride. They were caught in a sudden snow storm and the plane crashed, killing everyone on board.

When my sister didn't arrive home for the Thanksgiving holiday, my family and I didn't know what had happened. We had no idea that she had gone on that ill-fated plane ride. The wreckage of the plane wasn't discovered for a week. This was a very trying and traumatic time for my family and me as we and the police tried to piece together her disappearance. When the ordeal was finally over, we were never able to get any closure after her death. As a result, my family went through many years of unresolved grief.

That night in our living room, as I watched the program about the supernatural and saw how families were able to talk with their deceased loved ones, I thought that I could talk with my sister, and maybe even my cousin. The families told how they were finally able to get closure over their loved one's death, and I wanted that same closure.[2]

I had never seen anything about the supernatural before and was glued to the TV for the rest of the program. Something about what they were saying seemed strange, but I quickly dismissed the feeling I had. After all, nothing blatantly seemed wrong about wanting to talk with my sister one more time. After the program was over, I couldn't stop thinking about it.

The images of the families on the program who were helped stayed with me for several days. The program intrigued me. The thought that I was watching a program straight from Satan never entered my mind. At this point in my life, I didn't really understand that the devil even existed or that he could manifest himself as an angel of light.[3]

The Psychic Fair

My corporate job and my boyfriend consumed my time. Although I was extremely busy, the emptiness inside me continued to grow. After I saw the program on the supernatural, I began having reoccurring dreams that puzzled me. I often awoke in the middle of them. In the dream, I saw a light and knew the light was a Christian church. However, it seemed very different than the church I grew up in. I knew I was supposed to go to this church, but I didn't know how to find it. I heard the words, "Go to church and worship Me." After waking up one night after this dream, I thought, *How do I find this place?* I felt that the people in that church knew something I didn't, and if I could find this church, I would gain an understanding of something I needed to know.

The dreams troubled me. I described them to my boyfriend and asked, "Where do you think I should go?" Of course, he didn't have any more of a clue than I did. Neither one of us went to *any* church. But to help me in my spiritual search, a friend bought me a deck of tarot cards and taught me how to use them. At that time, I had no idea that tarot cards were a tool of the devil.

My job required that I travel a lot. One time I flew out of town to work on a video shoot for a Fortune 500 company. Because it was a long video shoot, I had to stay over through Monday. After we wrapped everything up on Friday, a coworker befriended me and showed me around her city for the weekend.

As we got to know each other, I shared some personal details about my life with her. I told her about my sister's death and how I felt I was searching for a greater meaning in my life. I also told her about the dreams I was having. As she listened, her face lit up and suggested we go to a psychic fair that was being held that weekend. "A psychic fair? What's that?" I asked. She laughed at me and couldn't believe I didn't know what a psychic fair was. I felt embarrassed but asked again.

"Psychics," she explained, "are people who have a gift that enables them to talk to loved ones who died." She told me that psychics are similar to counselors but they guide people using the spirit realm. She went to them from time to time and they gave her guidance for her life. She felt that they helped her a lot. She thought that maybe my sister had a message for me about what I was searching for in my life. She also thought I could get some spiritual advice on my career and boyfriend.

I remembered the television program about the supernatural. *Well, I thought, now I know the official word for it: psychic. Why not?* I thought, *What harm could there be in seeing a psychic?* I agreed to go.

My First Encounter

The psychic fair was located in a meeting room of a nice hotel. In the past, I had travelled to professional conferences at similar hotels. Nothing looked strange or weird. We each paid a $20 fee at the registration desk. When our names were called, a greeter escorted us to our separate readings.

The room accommodated approximately 10 tables, each with a very normal-looking person seated at the head of his or her table. There was no incense burning and no music playing. There was nothing abnormal about anything I saw. It looked similar to professional conferences I had attended.

I sat down for my reading. I studied the woman sitting across from me. She looked to be about 50 years old and was average in every way. She had graying hair, wore very little make-up, and dressed similar to how a schoolteacher or a government office worker might dress. Nothing about her appearance or demeanor made me feel uneasy. In fact, her appearance made me feel as though she was competent and experienced. She asked if I had ever met with a psychic before. I told her I hadn't.

To make me feel more comfortable, the psychic explained a little bit about how she worked. She told me her brother was a trained, licensed psychotherapist, and they often worked together in helping guide people through healing or finding their way in life. Knowing about her brother's profession made me feel as though she had more credibility. She then told me about her many years of experience. She said she felt called of God to be a psychic. I relaxed a little more and hoped I had found the spiritual help I was looking for.

The psychic used some of the same words the TV program and my coworker used, like angel guides, spiritual energy, and connecting to the universe. I didn't think much of this new language. I assumed it was a different way to explain the same spiritual truths I learned in church while growing up.

She asked me what questions I was seeking answers for. I explained that I liked my job, but I felt like there was something more I was supposed to do with my life. I told her about my inner search and emptiness. We talked about my boyfriend and I asked what she thought about him. I wanted to know if we should get married. I shared how my sister had died and told the psychic I wanted to talk with her if that was possible.

Surprising Guidance

The psychic didn't say much about my sister. Instead, she told me I was *not* supposed to marry the man I was with. She surprised me by telling me that I wasn't in the right job either. She said that I had "spiritual gifts" and I should follow a spiritual path instead. I was taken aback by her guidance. I wanted to marry the man I was with and I liked my job. I didn't know what she meant when she said I had "spiritual gifts." I had never heard of anything like that before. She explained that every major city has classes on psychic training, meditation, and inner healing. She suggested that when I got back home, I should find out where classes were in my city and get started right away. Her voice was filled with excitement and urgency.

I had no idea the guidance the psychic received came from evil spirits. Never once did she use terminology like demons or Satan. Instead, she used words like "spirit realm," "inner healing," and "universal spirit." This was a new, exotic language for God that I'd never heard before. Her words were like arrows that penetrated my heart. She spoke to every private desire I had. During my session, I literally felt as though an invisible magnet was pulling me toward this woman. It was such a strong sensation, not physical, and definitely not mental. I didn't know what it was, but it was tangible.

As I looked at the psychic, I thought how wonderful it must be to help people get healed and to help them get to know God better. As I watched her, I thought that what she was doing with her life was more valuable than what I was doing. I was just making training videos for corporations! I thought this might be the direction I needed to finally get my life on the right path. And maybe if I followed a spiritual path, my emptiness would go away.

An Inner Warning

After my reading, although I felt encouraged, I had a nagging feeling that something was strange. In hindsight, I can see that the Holy Spirit was trying to warn me against going down this path. However, I overrode my gut feeling since I couldn't put my finger on what was bothering me.[4] As my coworker drove me back to my hotel room, we talked about what the psychics told each of us. I didn't tell her about the uncomfortable feeling I had. She didn't seem to have the same concern, so I dismissed mine. I didn't want to feel embarrassed again. I wanted to be modern and worldly like she was, so I agreed with what she was saying. I asked her how to find classes in psychic development and meditation. She told me that most cities have classes like that in community centers. She had even taken some.

I decided as soon as I got home from my trip, enrolling in classes would be a top priority. I figured it couldn't be too hard to find out where classes were held. Looking back, I now realize that Satan was stealing everything I had in my life: my career, my boyfriend, and my real spiritual calling. He deceived me into thinking that his counterfeit version was better. And I fell for it.

---

[1] *"As the cloud is consumed and vanisheth away: so he that goeth down to the grave shall come up no more. He shall return no more to his house, neither shall his place know him any more"* (Job 7:9-10).

[2] *"For the living know that they shall die: but the dead know not any thing..."* (Ecclesiastes 9:5).

[3] *"... Satan himself is transformed into an angel of light"* (2 Cor. 11:14).

[4] *"My people are destroyed for lack of knowledge..."* (Hosea 4:6).

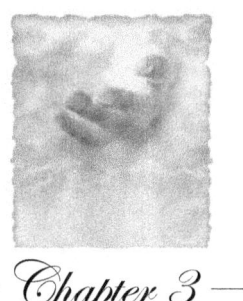

Chapter 3

BECOMING A PSYCHIC

By the time my flight landed back home, I was pulled into New Age like a magnet to metal. I grabbed hold of the psychic's words that I had "spiritual gifts." I thought that if I had a "gift," people would like me and want to be my friend. I believed that by having a gift, I would be accepted by people, and I could overcome the recurring rejection that I experienced since childhood.

When I look back, I can see how the devil manipulated me like a chess piece. He was easily able to do this without exposing who he was or that I was falling into a trap he had designed specifically for me. I had no Christian friends—no one to guide me in what the Bible said. And although my family was religious, they were just as uninformed about what I was getting into as I was. They couldn't warn me either.[1]

Soon after I had gotten home from my trip, I found a publication in the entrance of a grocery store that contained the class schedule for community education classes. There were classes on computer skills, art appreciation, and personal financial management. It also had an entire section on spiritual development classes. I thought, *Well, that sure was easy.*

I read and reread the class descriptions in the spiritual development section. I felt as though I was reading a menu from a five-star restaurant and couldn't choose which dessert I wanted—they all looked so good. The class descriptions used the same language the psychic used: inner healing, universal energy, spirit guides, and intuition development. Jesus wasn't mentioned but I didn't give much thought to it. I assumed this was a more hip, modern way to refer to God. As I read the descriptions, I felt the same hunger as I did watching the TV program on the supernatural. A spark of hope rose in me that maybe these classes could help me.

I was drawn to the class called "Intuition Development." It seemed like a good place to start. I read the biography of the instructor. She had been a professional social worker for 20 years. When I looked at her picture, I thought she looked like someone's friendly aunt. Eager to start, I signed up.

Learning the Ways of Satan

I was both nervous and curious when I went to the first class. It was held in an office building in downtown Minneapolis. Men and women of various ages attended the class. With the exception of a few hippies, everybody looked very normal. Looking at my class members, this could have been an accounting class.

When the instructor introduced herself, she captured my attention immediately. She went through her years of experience. And like the woman at the psychic fair, she felt God had called her to be a psychic, or as she preferred to call herself, an "intuitive," as she felt that term gave a higher dignity to the profession.

I liked her and eagerly attended all of her class sessions. I learned many new spiritual practices, like meditation, divination and how to connect to the spirit realm. The instructor introduced the class to exercises on how we could contact our own spirit guides. She let us know that she *always* worked with a spirit guide. Spirit guides were advanced spiritual beings that knew information that would help people here on earth. This was how she was guided through the spirit realm. She explained that some psychics like to work with tarot cards or astrology to obtain information for their clients or themselves. But she preferred to work with spirit guides who would tell her information directly. She explained that these spirit guides would be our friends for life. All we had to do was ask and they would readily serve us.

We were told that most beginners needed a "tool" like tarot cards, but as we advance in things the of the spirit realm, we can just work with our spirit guides. I wanted to get to the advanced level as quickly as possible. I didn't want to have to rely on tools. I wanted my own spirit guide. So I quickly registered for another class called "How to Connect With My Spirit Guide."

Uneasy Feelings

Periodically, I had an uneasy feeling about what I was doing. It was similar to the strange feeling I had after my first psychic reading. Although I recognized this uneasiness to be real, I didn't know what it was. I thought I would understand it when I was more "spiritually advanced." Then I remembered how uneasy I felt when I moved away from home to go to college. Eventually, I got accustomed to it. The same thing happened the first time I had to fly for a business trip. Although I was nervous during that first flight, eventually I got used to travelling. I thought this new spirituality would feel the same until I got used to it. I didn't realize that God was trying to speak to me.

I devoured everything my instructor taught, as well as the books she recommended. The more I learned, the more I was fascinated. The instructor even did partial readings for all of the students, which encouraged us to study further. During my reading, she told me that the "universal plan" for my life was to get married, have children, and serve people. That sounded pretty good to me, so I scheduled a full reading with her, which cost $60 for one hour. This reading led to more readings. I felt very fortunate to have gotten a mentor of her quality so quickly.

During my first year of study, I continually took classes. As soon as one class was over, I signed up for another. The more I studied, the more I wanted to teach others how to become an intuitive. When I looked at my class instructors, I thought, *That's what I'm going to do.* I remembered dreams I had as a little girl where I was standing in front of groups of people teaching them about God. I often tried to push those images out of my mind, but they always came back. Inside my heart, I always knew that was what I was supposed to do with my life. And since all of my instructors said they believed they were "called of God," I thought, *Maybe this is how I'm supposed to teach others about God.*

All of my classes focused on inner healing and helping people. One night as I was leaving one of my classes, I said to myself, *This is it. I've found my purpose in life.* As soon as I said those words, something on the inside said, *No, this isn't it.* What I was doing seemed right from the outside. Inwardly, I knew that something was wrong, but I didn't want to admit it to myself. None of the other people in the class seemed to think that anything was wrong with what we were being taught. So I again dismissed the feelings I was having.

Stepping Out As a Psychic

I started working toward getting a Master's Degree in Social Work hoping to change careers. I thought this would be a good counterpart to my new goal of becoming a psychic. The teacher I studied under had done this. I thought, *If it worked for her, maybe it would work for me.* Throughout the next year, I met a new group of people and made many friends, each on their own "spiritual search." Most of my new friends were professional, well educated, seemingly balanced, very normal people. We met for lunch and discussed which class or "healer" we wanted to go to next. Sometimes we even practiced doing readings for each other, utilizing the new skills we gained.

Using the meditation exercises I learned in class, I practiced connecting to my spirit guides every day. Within the year, I became so proficient that some of my friends referred their friends to me for readings. I was now able to "hear" specific words, like the names of family members and cities of birth when giving readings. I was encouraged to start charging money for the readings I was giving. My friends also told me that whenever I wanted to start teaching a class, they would pay to learn from me.

Success and Shambles

The success I was beginning to taste in New Age was a far cry from the rejection I often experienced while growing up. In New Age, I received love and acceptance. Satan knew exactly what would hook me and had worked for years to set up this trap. I wasn't seeking money or a position. I wanted and needed love. The love and encouragement I received from the New Age world kept drawing me in further. I was finally getting the love that I desperately wanted, and I was willing to do anything to keep it.

As the New Age side of my life was taking off, everything else was falling apart. My career was spiraling downward and my relationship with my boyfriend was in shambles. Eventually, my boyfriend and I broke up. Our breakup opened a lot of old wounds. I was devastated when my boyfriend rejected me and took our breakup hard. Not only did I lose someone I had hoped to marry, I also lost my home, friendships, money, and identity. I became depressed, and I stayed in bed for days. I felt like a complete failure and utterly discarded by life.

To me, the only thing I had left was New Age and the friends I had made through it. During my time of grief and isolation, I devoured as many books on astrology, mysticism, and divination that I could get a hold of. I thought that if I completely immersed myself in becoming a psychic, I would find my purpose in life. New Age became my salvation, and I wanted to surrender my life to this apparent calling. After a few weeks, I picked myself up and angrily purposed myself to move on with my life.

Thoughts of committing suicide began to flood my mind as they had on and off throughout my life. This time, however, the thoughts consumed me with a greater viciousness. It felt like a choke hold. I remembered my cousin who had taken his life. I thought, *This is how my cousin must have felt before he ended his life.* He was such a good person, and I was sure he had to be in heaven. Through my studies in New Age, I began to believe that reincarnation might be true. If so, suicide could be my way out. I felt driven to do anything I could to find relief from being ravaged by this blackness. I thought I could check out of this life and take my chances on what I would come back as in my next life.

As I contemplated ending my life, a figure of light appeared to me.[2] Although I could not see His facial features, I knew it was Jesus. I was alarmed and afraid. I didn't understand what was happening. By now, I was becoming accustomed to spiritual visitations by "angels." However, this was different. I knew this was God, who I had been taught about as a little girl. He came to warn me against committing suicide.

"Don't do it," He sternly warned. I looked at Him in shock. It felt as though His love punctured through Satan's death grip on me. I knew Jesus was stronger than anything I was dealing with. He also warned me against going into New Age and becoming a psychic.

Suddenly, I saw into the spirit realm. On the one side was the realm of God. It was filled with light. Then off to another side, I saw New Age. It looked dead, gray, and dirty. I didn't understand what I was seeing. At that time, Jesus didn't reveal to me that Satan was in charge of New Age or that I was interacting with demons. However, I clearly saw that New Age was not of God.

However, I was heartbroken because of the breakup with my boyfriend. I was angry and blamed God for the pain I was experiencing. I wanted someone else to hurt the same way I was hurting, so I took it out on Jesus. I aimed my anger and rejection back at Him and pushed Him away. I said to Him, "I want to do this for awhile. Then I'll come back to you." I felt a flash of His anger and then surprisingly, I felt a deep sorrow in Him that struck me in my gut. Since I wouldn't receive Him, there was nothing more He could do. Suddenly, He was gone.[3]

I was shocked that Jesus abruptly left. I knew He loved me. My heart raced. *Why did He leave?* Although I didn't understand it at the time, Jesus was grieving because He knew what was about to happen to me. I was going to have to learn the hard way.

This encounter frightened me, and I tried to push it out of my mind. I reasoned to myself that everything would be okay, even though I knew I had made a wrong choice. This visitation kept me from committing suicide, but it didn't keep me from becoming a psychic. I then proceeded down a path that would eventually lead to my destruction.

I did everything I could to justify my behavior. I surrounded myself with people who were deceiving themselves as well. I had hoped their voices would drown out the voice of my conscience. I think there is an unspoken rule about sin. You can make yourself feel better in a crowd of people who are doing the same thing. Somehow you can justify your behavior, although the nagging feeling in your conscience never goes away. But no matter what you do, you can't alter the truth. So I deceived myself.

Over the next several days and weeks, I began having terrible spiritual experiences. It felt as though God's hand of protection had been lifted off of me. I didn't know it, but my choice gave Satan free reign in my life. A darkness came over me that was frightening. I felt as though I was being struck and physically hurt by what I thought were my new angels. Mental torment wasn't new to me, but it seemed as though it had been ratcheted up. And in spite of everything that was happening, I pretended that I was in control.

I had several mentors who helped me transition into being a psychic. I continued working part-time in the corporate world, but studied and taught on the evenings and weekends. I began teaching psychic development classes for the same organization that I first learned from. They even placed a picture of me on the cover of their promotional catalog to advertise their classes.

Immersed in New Age

Doors of opportunity to teach and speak seemed to fly open. At this point, Satan was calling the shots, and I was walking out his plan. I taught psychic development at well-known coffee shops, bookstores, a university, and various health and healing expos. I was interviewed by several radio stations. An opportunity to possibly appear on a New Age television program even opened up, although in the end I decided against it. My work as a psychic exploded so quickly that I had a hard time balancing my part-time job with being a psychic.

I spent several thousands of dollars buying New Age and world religions books. If the book had "god" in it, I bought it, although I excluded books on Christianity. I was determined to understand Hinduism, Buddhism, Native American spirituality, psychic development, astrology, and the history of all the world religions. If it had to do with religion and spirituality, I studied it—the entire time over-riding my conscience.

None of the books I purchased or the classes I attended had any warning labels on them: "Caution: May Result in Demon Possession." The words "Satan" or demons were never mentioned. At this time, I didn't understand that Satan, demons, or hell were real. Even though I didn't understand the Gospel message, I knew I rebelled against God after Jesus appeared to me. I thought if I tried hard enough to do things my own way, I could make everything turn out all right. I later found out that doesn't work. You can never go against God and still have things turn out right.

When I would come across teachings of Jesus, I read them too, but if it conflicted with my new world view that "all roads lead to God," I would set it aside. I never bought a Bible. None of my teachers believed in salvation, sin, or hell. They believed in Jesus, but equated Him with other great spiritual teachers throughout time, like Buddha, the Dalai Lama, and Mahatma Gandhi. Because I was surrounded by people who didn't believe in heaven or hell, I began rejecting what I had been taught as a child and allowed myself to slide into believing the same things. All of my spiritual teachers believed they were chosen by God to help humanity and that they were laying their lives down for a high calling. It wasn't long before I began to believe this to. Through this erosion process, my conscience became seared.[4]

For the most part, I was very successful in New Age. However, there were some bumps along the way. Like the time I was being interviewed on a prominent, nationally syndicated news station. The interviewer had been a client, although at the time I didn't know who she was. After the reading, she asked if she could interview me for her radio news program. She also wanted me to do a partial reading for her on the radio. She thought it would be great for her audience to hear. At the time, I was thrilled at the opportunity.

However, during the interview, it seemed as though a fog came over me. I had never had this happen before when I was doing a reading. I could not perform her psychic reading, and I couldn't answer any of her questions. She became frustrated and promptly ended the interview saying it was unusable material.

I believe God intervened, shutting this opportunity down. If this interview had been successful, national opportunities could have resulted with other news programs. Although I was embarrassed because I blew that interview, now I'm so grateful it turned out that way. Who knows where I would be today if God didn't block it.

---

[1] *"But there were also false prophets among the people, just as there will be false teachers among you. They will secretly introduce destructive heresies, even denying the sovereign Lord who bought them—bringing swift destruction on themselves. Many will follow their shameful ways and will bring the way of truth into disrepute. In their greed these teachers will exploit you with stories they have made up. Their condemnation has long been hanging over them, and their destruction has not been sleeping"* (2 Peter 2:1-3 NIV).

[2] *"To whom shall I speak, and give warning, that they may hear? behold, their ear is uncircumcised, and they cannot hearken: behold, the word of the Lord is unto them a reproach; they have no delight in it"* (Jeremiah 6:10).

[3] *"And even as they did not like to retain God in their knowledge, God gave them over to a reprobate mind, to do those things which are not convenient; Being filled with all unrighteousness. . ."* (Romans 1:28-29).

[4] *"For if a man think himself to be something, when he is nothing, he deceiveth himself"* (Galatians 6:3). *"Speaking lies in hypocrisy; having their conscience seared with a hot iron"* (1 Timothy 4:2).

Chapter 4

ONE WRONG TURN AFTER ANOTHER

Other doors of opportunity kept opening for me in New Age. I was thrilled to connect with a large New Age book publisher. We talked about me coming on board and working for them. The position with the book publisher would have given me many more opportunities to speak. Instead of simply being a regional speaker, I would have had a national audience. Once on a national scale, television opportunities would open up. I had already been approached by one organization to appear as a guest on their television program. If things kept progressing, on the path I was on, I would have advanced into being a New Age "televangelist". The book publisher was very interested in hiring me. In fact, everyone I talked to during the interview process said I was exactly who they wanted.

The book publisher assured me that the position wouldn't interfere with my work as a psychic. In fact, my "spirituality" was an asset for this position, as my work and beliefs mirrored the beliefs represented in their publications. I was even promised help in publishing my first book. My position would connect me to all the right people I needed to get published, from writing and editing to graphic designers. Most importantly, I would connect to critical marketing avenues to get my book publicized.

The possibility of working for this publisher greatly interested me. After the interview, the director of the editorial department along with two book editors walked me to the lobby. My mind raced with excitement at the opportunity I had in front of me. I thought, *Could this be true? I'm going to be a published author . . . and help so many people!* This was my dream about to come true. When we reached the lobby, I saw a bookcase that displayed the publisher's current publications. As I looked at the book covers, the first titles I noticed had beautiful images on them, much in the same way I envisioned my book to look like. The titles of these books used words like "intuition," "healing," and "angels." I stirred with excitement looking at the books. My interviewers just smiled as they observed my obvious interest. I felt like a child who had just received a brand new, shiny red bicycle.

The Ugly Side of New Age

My interviewers again told me they encouraged their staff to write books. It was one of the benefits of working at the publishing house. I was trying to take all of this in as I continued looking at their product line. Then I noticed books that had very disturbing images on their covers. These books had dark covers with snakes, pentagrams, and other frightening images on them. And the titles used words like "witchcraft," "occult," and "wizards."

Trying to hide my disapproval, I turned to my interviewers and asked, "You publish books like this too?" My question surprised them as they looked at each other and then at me. Finally, one of them responded to my naïve question, "They are all the same. Don't you understand that?"

My Final Warning

At that moment, a voice resonated inside my entire being, "If you go any further, you're not coming back." It was the same voice that had warned me to not get involved in New Age years earlier. I knew it was Jesus Christ speaking to me. He was warning me one last time. However, I was alarmed by the seriousness with which this warning reverberated within me. This was not like the conversation I had with Jesus when He first appeared to me. The nagging feeling I had that what I was doing was wrong suddenly overpowered me. I knew beyond a shadow of a doubt that I was living a lie and I couldn't ignore it anymore.

I tried to hide my fear and politely ended the conversation. I shook their hands and nearly ran out of the building. When I reached my car, I was shaking so badly that I could barely get the key in the lock to open the door. I don't know what I was trying to run away from faster, the publishing house or the voice of God.

Again, I heard God's voice resonate within me. "If you go any further, you are not coming back." I wrestled with my self-deception. I was face-to-face with the choice I had made with my life. I could no longer push away the memory of Jesus appearing to me and warning me about being involved in New Age and becoming a psychic. I remembered the scene of how New Age was dark and separated from God. And then I remembered how I rejected His warning.

As I sat in my car, I had to force myself to start the engine and pull out of the parking lot. And as I was driving away from what I thought was one of the greatest opportunities of my life, I made one of the most critical decisions I had ever made. I decided to walk away from the psychic world even though it had become my primary source of income. Immediately I felt the urgency lift from me. With my decision made, I breathed a sigh of relief. I thought that I could just walk away from this part of my life and everything would be okay.

Attacked by Forces of Evil

When I was a psychic, I didn't believe Satan existed or that I was serving him. Even though God showed me what I was doing was involved in darkness, I never associated it with the devil. However, just because I didn't believe in Satan and evil spirits didn't mean they weren't real. As quickly as I made the decision to leave the psychic world, another horror—unlike anything I had ever experienced—came upon me.

Suddenly my car filled with pure evil. I saw dark, transparent figures swirling around me. I felt something claw at me. It was similar to what I had experienced as a little girl but magnified many times over. I was so terrified I could barely drive. I don't know how I made it back to my apartment without crashing the car into something. I hoped that if I could get to my apartment and close the door, everything would be okay. But once inside, the evil around me only intensified.

More evil was waiting for me inside my apartment. Although it was midday, it seemed as though all of the light had been sucked out of my apartment. Tangible fear gripped me until I could hardly breathe. I felt as though I was being choked and was fearful that I would die.

Evil, ugly creatures began appearing around me. Their eyes were fiery red and filled with hatred. Their claw-like hands had no flesh on them. The creatures were transparent, yet black as thick oil. Each had different bodies and different features. All were grotesque. Out of them came shrieks and groans that were not from this world.

Somehow I knew these creatures "owned" me because I had been a psychic. And they weren't going to let me leave their domain. I cried out to my spirit guides to help me. None answered. Neither did any of the "gods" I had studied come to my rescue. I realized that I had gotten myself into something I couldn't get out of.

Rescued by God

The creatures were filled with rage and violence. One look at their faces and I knew they were bent on destroying me. They kept circling around me, and no matter where I went, I couldn't escape. When I felt them physically and spiritually clutch and grab me, I cried out, "God! Help me! Oh, please help me!" At that moment, a great light flashed down on me. The creatures shrieked and crawled away from the powerful presence that filled the room. Although I felt God's presence for several days, I could still see the red, evil eyes hungrily watching me. When I went to sleep, I saw those eyes, and when I woke up, they were still there.

Because I didn't believe in Satan or demons, I didn't understand that the creatures I saw were demons. I didn't realize that I had opened myself up to them by becoming a psychic. And of course, I wasn't a born again Christian at that time, so I didn't know yet that any Christian could immediately stop this kind of demonic attack by using the name of Jesus.

The presence of evil lessened over the next several weeks. Although I was determined to leave the psychic world, I was still booked to teach a spiritual development class and could not get out of my commitment. However, on my way to teach a class, I was in a head-on collision with another vehicle. I was only moderately injured but wasn't able to work for several months. I was so relieved that my remaining classes had to be cancelled. Finally my time as a psychic was over.

BEING SPIRITUAL AND SINNING?

As I was recovering from the car crash, I transitioned back into working in the corporate world. Over the course of time, I made a new friend who was in New Age but also believed in Jesus Christ. One time she said to me, "It's time to accept Jesus as your teacher." Even though she didn't really understand salvation, God used her to start pointing me in the right direction. In my heart, I knew Jesus was the help that I needed. And I reasoned that this was more of the truth than what I had been following. I knew for sure that I could no longer be a psychic, but I thought I could still believe in some parts of New Age.

One of the things I liked about New Age was that I felt I could be spiritual and sin at the same time. I wanted to live like the world lived and have immoral relationships. All of my friends did this before they got married. But from my upbringing, I knew this was wrong. I remembered thinking one time, *With New Age, I can have God and still sin.*

And now, I knew in my heart if I completely left New Age, I couldn't date the way I did. To put it plainly, I wouldn't be able to have sex before marriage. I had convinced myself that I could stop working as a psychic and that would be enough. And I would still believe some very mild New Age beliefs, like meditation, inner healing, yoga, and so forth. I would believe in Jesus, too, but at a distance. But God was really dealing with my heart and spoke to me in a way that I very much knew was Him.

I needed to choose between having boyfriends or being "married" to one Jesus and living a pure life. I am embarrassed to say, I rejected Jesus at this time too. Although I didn't want to share this information, I did so because I believe many people make the same decision. I included this information so people can see the consequence of making this choice.

Even after God had supernaturally protected me from the evil, wicked creatures that had surrounded me, I rejected Jesus. Not because I didn't want to follow after Him because I did. I just wanted to be able to sin *and* have a relationship with Him. I wanted to have Jesus on my own terms. And with God, you can't do that.

Another Wrong Road

My friend told me about the church she was attending. Her church combined some of Jesus' teachings with New Age. She thought I might enjoy it. I went to a church service and liked it. Essentially, I got what I wanted. This church taught that you could believe in Jesus on your own terms. I attended this church for approximately two years.

During the time I attended the New Age church, I began working full time in the corporate world again. While life on the outside was better and normal again, my private life was anything but normal. I had times where I was happy, but I still experienced episodes of darkness. And when the darkness came on me, it seemed to overtake me. Now it was much worse than when I was a child.

While I never again experienced the permeation of evil to the degree I did upon my decision to stop being a psychic, the creatures of darkness never completely left me. It seemed as though they came and went as they pleased. As a result, I experienced frightful torments at their will. Grief or fear often gripped my mind. Sometimes the creatures came into my bedroom at night, and the fear that came on me was paralyzing. There was nothing I could do about it. I felt as though I was being stalked by an evil presence. And I didn't know what to do. I thought if I told anyone, they would think that I was crazy. When this happened, I only wanted to end my life so I would be free of the torment.

My Life Was Falling Apart

Even though I began to make a high income, somehow I would lose everything I earned. My relationships with men were what I wouldn't give up for God, but none of them worked out. I also began to get sick, and the doctors couldn't help me. One time, for no medical reason, half my hair fell out. Another time, my eyes became red and swollen and wouldn't stop tearing whenever I tried to wear contacts.

I also developed a fatigue disorder that couldn't be diagnosed. At times, all of my energy left me. At these times, I didn't have enough strength to get out of bed to eat or shower. I would just have to wait until my energy came back and I could function on a day-to-day basis. I felt as though I was a puppet, but I didn't know who was pulling the strings. Even though these were physical illnesses, I knew the cause was spiritual. And because I had a spiritual problem, I didn't know who to turn to for help.

I went to medical doctors, but they couldn't help me. So as insane as this sounds, I went to psychics for help! Somehow I thought they could free me from the darkness. They told me that this was the "price" I had to pay for having a gift from God. Some even said they suffered from similar issues.

I tried a psychologist. After multiple sessions and hundreds of dollars, I became angry during a session. I interrupted her and said, "My problem is spiritual. *Can you help me?*" She struggled for an answer but didn't have one. She told me she didn't know how to give me what I was asking for. I never went back to her.

One day, the creatures with red eyes came back and attacked me. I feared for my life. The next day, I went to my New Age pastor. He told me he believed the fear I was experiencing was psychological and that I needed to be more "kind and loving to myself." He said the long-held Christian belief that Satan is real was outdated and that we don't need to be under that bondage anymore. He believed God was a loving being who supports the choices we make. Although he had a Bible on his desk, he only believed the "essence" of it. He said he didn't quote from it often because he believes it's spiritually abusive to call people sinners.

Eventually, I left the New Age church because things weren't any better there than when I was a psychic. I tried everything to get help. My pastor couldn't help me. Doctors and psychologists couldn't help me. The psychics couldn't help me. On my quest to find health and healing, I spent $50,000 trying to get well. But the oppressive darkness never left.

Over the course of my time in New Age, I dated many different men. Instead of finding love, I went from one bad relationship to another. It seemed as though I was drawn to men who would use me, control me, and then reject me. The last man I dated was particularly brutal. When he ended our relationship, I felt crushed and discarded. And that's what finally pushed me over the edge. I couldn't go on living like this. So I decided to end my life.

Chapter 5

PLANNING MY SUICIDE

> *"When we were utterly helpless, Christ came at just the right time and died for us sinners."*
>
> —Romans 5:6 (NLT)

"Mom, I'm going to commit suicide." Although this was not the first time I had talked to my mother about ending my life, this time I intended to go through with it.

Mom and I talked about heaven and hell and wondered if they were real places. We talked about God and wondered if He was real too. I remember saying, "I don't know if there is a heaven or a hell or how to meet God. *If* there is a God, I will finally meet Him, one way or another." Even though Jesus had appeared to me years earlier, I had studied so many world religions, that Jesus got lumped in with all of the other gods. Eventually, I reached a point where I didn't know what was true and if there really was a God.

Throughout our conversation nothing my mother said could change my mind. Anytime she offered me some kind of reason to live, I kept countering, "Something is very wrong with my life and I don't know what else to do. Once and for all, I just want to meet God." I didn't want my parents to be plagued with any guilt over my death. I told my mother that she and my father had been great parents and my death would not be their fault.

My mother didn't really believe that I was going to go through with taking my life, or she would have come to my home to intervene. She thought that this conversation was no different from the countless hours she had spent encouraging me on the phone over the years.

Eventually, we said good-bye. We told each other that we loved each other and hung up the phone.

Not the End, But a New Beginning

Although it has been many years since that phone call, I can vividly remember that day as though it were yesterday. I was staring at my own death, preferring an uncertain afterlife to the darkness that filled my soul. I had taken several days off from my job to make the final arrangements for my death. I intended to end my life through asphyxiation. My plan was to seal off the garage, turn on my car, and sit in it until I died, painlessly.

Although I had a detailed plan on how I was going to kill myself, after I said good-bye to my mother, I kept going in circles. I remember holding my head, trying to force my brain to think. But then something unexpected happened. A figure that radiated gold light walked up to me and said, "Everything you think that can only heal when you die, I can help you with here. You just have to say 'yes' to me." (See graphic: Surrendering to Jesus.)

I stared at this figure and shook my head. I believed I was seeing things and thought that at any moment this mirage would disappear. I remember thinking, *Now on top of everything else, I've completely lost my mind.* I stared into the golden light and the man was still there.

"Jesus, is that you?" I asked. He stretched His hand out to me.[1] I couldn't make out his exact features because of the light that emanated from His being. Yet, I somehow knew in my heart that Jesus was standing before me. He repeated, "Everything that you think can only heal when you die, I can help you with here. You just have to say 'yes' to me."[2]

I was trying to understand what was happening. I knew I wasn't dreaming and that what I was seeing was very real.[3] It reminded me of a time when I almost had a car accident. I was driving home in a blizzard in the middle of winter when I suddenly lost control of my car and it began sliding back and forth across the icy road. Each second seemed like it was stretched while I was trying to make life or death decisions as my car swerved through multiple lanes of rush hour traffic.

And now as I was hovering between life and death, the seconds seemed to tick slower, as if they were carrying the weight of my decision to end my life. Moments earlier, I told my mother that I wanted to be with God. And now, as Jesus stood before me, I realized that my prayer had been answered. My plans for death were jerked out from under me by this unexpected turn of events. I had been prepared to die, but I didn't know if I was prepared to live.

I looked at Jesus and said, "Yes."[4]

Here was Jesus who I had rejected so many times in my life coming to me once again. He reached toward me and literally touched me inside my head with his hand. When He did that, it felt as though something snapped and lifted off of my mind. I knew that Jesus was touching not only my body, but He was also reaching into my spirit and removing the darkness. It felt as though He reached into my broken heart and touched who I was. With His touch, I could see darkness lift off of me. And when the darkness left, the desire to die left too.

Healing, Learning, and Growing

For the next several days, I experienced things I did not understand. A golden light seemed to surround me. It wasn't a natural light that you could see with your physical eyes. Jesus, the light of the world[5] was with me. At times, I saw Jesus as I had in those first moments. At other times, I did not see Him but was very conscious of His presence.

Soon after my initial encounter with Christ, I called my mom. I wanted to let her know that I was going to be okay. When she answered the phone, I blurted, "Mom, I'm not going to commit suicide. And I think I've just met Jesus!"

Of course, she didn't understand what I was talking about. My conversation was short, but at least she was relieved that my latest suicidal episode was over. I told her that I was going to rest and that I would call her soon.

Prying Open My Wounded Heart

During this remarkable time with Jesus, I felt as though I was in a safe refuge. As the reality of what I was experiencing sunk in, I looked at Jesus and was amazed that here was Jesus Christ, the son of God, in my home!

Opening my heart to Jesus was difficult. In many ways, I acted the same way an abandoned or abused animal reacts when it has been captured by a rescue organization. Because the animal has been mistreated for so long, it no longer trusts people. Although it is now safe, it trembles and shrinks back into the corner of its cage, trying to get away from the very help that will enable it to recover. The animal desperately wants food and attention but not at the cost of being abused again. But because Jesus could look deep within my soul, He was able to see a faint desire to live. And He stayed with me until He could coax that glimmer of hope into a burning flame. Here He was with me again, the same way He was when He warned me against becoming a psychic. I resisted the memory of how I had rejected Him. I certainly had learned the hard way.

When I forced myself to open my heart, it felt as though a fresh wound had been scraped. I had deceived myself and had been deceived so many times through New Age. I had tried to convince myself that I was following the truth. Now here I was, in the presence of the Truth, the only real God. Being in His presence stripped away the layers of confusion in my mind until all that was left was what was true. As this happened, I was filled with shame. How could He take me back?

Looking at Jesus with fear, hope, and shame, I said, "You are *God*, aren't you?" Without Him saying a word, I knew that He was the son of God and everything was going to be okay. A deep peace quieted my tired soul. I knew then that the spiritual treadmill I was on finally stopped. I knew that none of the other gods of the world religions I had studied had showed up to save me. Buddha didn't come. The Native American Great Spirit didn't come. No Hindu god came. Allah didn't come. And no New Age spirit guide came. Only Jesus came to my rescue. What a fool I had been. I thought, *How different things would have been if only I had received Him the first time He came to me.*

A Partial Instead of Complete Deliverance

"If you are God," I said to Jesus, "you can heal me of my problem. And if you are able to heal me, I will serve you the rest of my life, and I will do whatever you ask me to do." I didn't understand then that my "problem" was that I was possessed by demons.

Although the intensity of the spirit of suicide immediately left me, a heaviness still remained attached to my soul. Jesus told me it was possible for me to be completely healed. However, I had hurt for such a long time that I told Jesus I didn't believe that could happen. I knew this made Him sad, and He asked me again if I wanted to be completely healed. I told Him I was afraid, and I didn't see how it was possible. Jesus then explained that my deliverance would take several years. Eventually, I would become completely free, but I would go through a process of "partial deliverances."

Jesus didn't want to frighten me or push Himself on me in any way. Because I couldn't believe that Jesus could help me fully and completely, my faith hindered what God could have done in my life at that time.

Pure Love

Being in Jesus' presence, I began to remember all of the chances He had given me throughout my life. One time while I was teaching a psychic class in a popular bookstore, a young girl came to one of my classes. I thought she was a student. After I had finished teaching, she came up and introduced herself. After we exchanged introductions, she began telling me that Jesus loved me and wanted to be my best friend. I remember gritting my teeth and thinking, *Another Jesus freak!* I thought she was very sweet but very deceived and closed-minded. I was frustrated that I couldn't get her to stop talking as I kept trying to politely end the conversation.

Another time, years prior to my being involved in New Age, a pastor witnessed to me on a street corner. He gave me a tract on salvation. I remembered looking at him and being afraid. I saw a bright light around him. In the presence of that light, I became aware of my own darkness. It unnerved me. I walked away from him as quickly as I could. (Years later, I supernaturally met this pastor again at a church the Lord sent me to. I served in his street evangelism ministry. He was instrumental in training me for the Lord's call on my life.)

But now that I was in Jesus' presence I thought, *I can't believe I walked away from pure love my entire life.* Although I had rejected Jesus so many times before, He readily and completely accepted me. I've learned that God is truth, and all lies are exposed in His presence. When I was in the presence of Jesus, there was no doubt in my mind that He was the son of God.

In New Age, I believed spirituality had to be hard and the search for God exotic. When I was in church as a child, I was afraid of God and viewed Him as a cold, judging, and distant old man. But Jesus was so simple and gentle to me. Being in the presence of Jesus, I saw the fullness of who God really was: love, spiritual strength, and power. Although I had been taught about God throughout my upbringing, I didn't understand that I could know Him like this.

I tried to act "right," in His presence, much in the same way you would act in front of an important dignitary—stiff, proper, and somewhat false. But instead, Jesus wanted the opposite. He wanted me to be who I really was. I had to remove all masks and come into His presence without any pretense. He only wanted me to feel safe and loved. He wanted to heal my heart. And the only way He could heal me from the reasons I wanted to commit suicide was by showing me that I didn't have to be anything but myself. He loved me just the way I was.

At one point, I was sitting on a couch in my home office. Jesus was standing off to the side of me. By now, I felt more comfortable with Him. I looked at Him and angrily asked, "If you loved me, why did you let all of 'this' happen in my life?" I was referring to all of the bad things that had happened throughout my life. As soon as the words left my lips, I feared He would be angry with me for being so forward. Immediately, I shrank back from His presence fearing rejection. Jesus wasn't surprised by my question. He already knew what I was thinking. He said there were things I didn't understand yet, but that I would learn why from the Bible later. I asked Him more questions when He was with me. Multiple times, He responded the same way.

Talking with Jesus reminded me of some of my favorite childhood memories with my mom. Whenever my mom and I talked, I knew she listened intently to my every word. I'd tell her about my day or some hurt I had experienced at school. My mother seemed to have endless reservoirs of attention for each of her children. She made me feel as though I was the only person in the world when I talked to her and that every one of my hurts or concerns was very important to her. It was that same way with Jesus. His entire focus was on me, and I knew He wanted me there with Him.

Eventually, Jesus began telling me what He wanted me to do with my life. At one point, He lifted up a Bible and said, "You'll teach from this book now." Suddenly the realization that the Bible was the *only* Word of God dropped inside of me. "The *Bible* is the truth?" I exclaimed. "Oh, that will make things a lot easier. I was really getting confused. I didn't know which book was right!"

Although I had studied nearly every world religion, instead of being enlightened, I was thoroughly confused. I was so glad to finally know what the truth really was and to admit the truth to myself.

---

[1] "... *the Lord's hand is not shortened, that it cannot save...*" (Isaiah 59:1). "... *And he said, Who ar thou, Lord? And the Lord said, I am Jesus...*" (Acts 9:5 KJV).

[2] "*For God so loved the world, that he gave his only begotten Son, that whosoever believeth in him should not perish, but have everlasting life...*" (John 3:16).

[3] "... *I will come to visions and revelations of the Lord*" (2 Corinthians 12:1).

[4] "*And I will give them a heart to know me, that I am the Lord: and they shall be my people, and I will be their God: for they shall return unto me with their whole heart*" (Jeremiah 24:7).

[5] "*I am the light of the world: he that followeth me shall not walk in darkness, but shall have the light of life*" (John 8:12).

Chapter 6

SEEING INTO THE SPIRIT REALM

"... the heavens were opened, and I saw visions of God."
—Ezekiel 1:1

During this beautiful time, I learned many things, and my eyes were opening to the truth of the Bible. Now that I understood who God really was, Jesus also wanted me to understand who Satan really was. It was if scales fell off my eyes.[1] But before this truth was revealed to me, Jesus made sure I knew He was fully in charge and that there was no need to be afraid.

I was sitting in the living room of my house. Jesus was next to me. I looked up and the spirit realm opened before my eyes. In the same way that I could see Jesus, I now saw a group of evil creatures.[2] (See graphic: Meeting My Demons.) When I saw the creatures, I fearfully looked at Jesus. Why was He doing this to me? Jesus nodded at me and let me know that everything was okay. "Just watch," He said as He pointed at the creatures. I had to trust Him as I watched the horrors of hell unfold before my eyes.

I was shocked at what I saw. The moment I looked at the evil-looking creatures, I realized they were demons. *If these creatures are demons,* I thought, *Satan and hell must be real too.* As the realization of this flooded my mind, I marveled at what I had just escaped. *Oh, God, hell is real. And I was just minutes from that place!* When the full impact of this hit me, I wanted to throw up! Jesus watched me with encouragement as He let the truth sink in.

I felt very uneasy as I watched. There were so many demons and only one Jesus. But He wasn't at all afraid of them. It was obvious that He was the one who was in charge in the spirit realm. When I looked at Jesus, He reminded me of a confident national leader at an official event. A quiet authority emanated from His being, and it was evident that each demon understood the power and authority that Jesus had. By watching the way He carried Himself, I knew I was in the presence of a King who wielded absolute power. I moved closer to Jesus and knew He would watch over and protect me.

Whenever Jesus spoke, His every word made the demons shudder. They quickly moved away from me like crocodiles slithering into a pond. When the Word of God was spoken from His lips, it was like a supernatural force came forth.

The demons stuck together in a group in the same way wild dogs or a pack of wolves do. They each were unique creatures with individual features, although some looked very similar to others. I was able to look directly into their faces and meet their eyes. It was like looking at a group of people, each with a distinct appearance, body, and personality. However, all light and good had been removed from the demons.[3] They were gray and dead looking. Only darkness, pure evil, and fear emanated from their beings. Although it was midday, all of the light in the room seemed to have been sucked out.

I was shocked when one of the demons stepped forward and began screeching at Jesus, "She's supposed to be here with us right now." The devil quickly retreated and rejoined the other demons. They were asking Jesus for me! I looked at Jesus and was afraid that He would turn me over to the demons.[4]

The demons were angry and howled as they paced back and forth. I had never seen such violent rage. They were enraged because they had carefully plotted events throughout my life trying to drive me to suicide. I froze when Jesus allowed me to understand that. *I had been scheduled to die and go to hell that day.* But Jesus cheated them of their victory!

I was speechless and horrified. But mostly, I was grateful. I realized that this was what Jesus had been trying to protect me from all along. I suddenly felt very small in His presence. And I felt ashamed that I had rejected Him all my life.

The All Powerful King

As I watched the demons' fear of Jesus, I saw a different side to Jesus' character. I had previously relaxed in His tenderness toward me. But now I also saw His strength and absolute, unquestioned authority. Jesus was King in the spirit realm and no other spiritual force had any power over Him. Jesus was entirely triumphant over these spirits of darkness.[5] I respected and reverenced Him, as well as loved Him. Jesus was a strong, but gentle teacher. He encouraged me every step of the way. He knew I needed to learn how to remain fearless and unimpacted in front of these hosts of hell.

My Tormentors Revealed

As I watched these demons, some of them seemed so familiar to me. It was as though I had known them for a long time. Then I realized that some of them had been tormenting me since I was a child. With disgust, I recognized others as my spirit guides. However, when I was in New Age, I thought they were angels. It was shocking to see what they really looked like. With my eyes opened to what my spirit guides really were, I turned to Jesus and asked, "If I wasn't serving God, who was I serving?" Jesus didn't need to answer. I looked at the demons and saw their proud, twisted smiles. I knew the answer to my question. Once again, I became nauseous.

One by one they stepped forward and "introduced" themselves. "I'm Suicide. I made you want to die!" it said with a perverted satisfaction. And it began describing how it had hovered over me like a dark cloud, whispering in my ear, "Go ahead, kill yourself." I was shocked when I finally realized that the darkness I had known was really this demon. Another said, "I'm Torment." Another said, "I'm Grief." Another, "I'm Rejection." I immediately saw how this demon had manipulated events in my life since childhood where people would use me and then throw me away.

I felt the demons' extreme hatred for me and their intense desire to have my soul. They were angry because they had almost gotten me for eternity. They acted like rabid dogs circling their prey, waiting for the right moment to attack. However, because of Jesus, they could not get beyond a certain point.

I looked in horror at the demons. Sadness and anger washed over me as I remembered the years of torment these devils had caused.

I was horrified as I watched the demons leave. With Jesus remaining at my side, I thought of how so much of my life had been stolen. However, I realized that everything I had wanted and searched for throughout my life, Jesus gave me in moments. He showed me the way out of the spiritual prison I thought I could never escape from.

Deceived No More!

I saw how these demons had successfully used rejection and low self-esteem as a weapon against me since I was a child. Repeated rejection crushed my self-esteem until I had no self-worth. I remembered how the first psychic I went to told me that I had "spiritual gifts." And then I realized that the "gifts" I thought I had weren't "gifts" at all. What I had was demons! However, I saw that the arrow Satan used to pierce my heart was the illusion of acceptance.

As Jesus allowed me to see these things, I was flooded with the truth: I didn't have to "do" anything or "be" somebody to receive Jesus' love and acceptance. He loved me just the way I was. I could have received Him years earlier and have gotten the real thing instead of being seduced by the counterfeit.

Seeing the Lost

Although I was shaken, Jesus wanted me to see one more thing. Suddenly another scene in the spirit realm opened up. (See graphic: The Lost.) I saw a sea of people and knew they were people who were currently living. Satan was tormenting many of them in similar ways that I had been tormented in my mind and body. As they walked, they stumbled and fell because blinders were on their eyes. They couldn't see clearly—only what the blinders allowed them to see. I also realized that these same blinders had been on me. The people were wrestling against demonic powers although they didn't understand what they were fighting. And no matter how hard they tried, they couldn't break free. It was painful to watch and not do anything to help them.

These people were not born again, nor did they know what salvation in Jesus Christ was. Because of the specific bondage each of them had,

Satan could manipulate them like puppets and make to do whatever he wanted.

It seemed as though demons "marked" certain people as their own. They would circle "their" person in the same way wolves circle their prey. Although the demons tried to kill the people, they couldn't. This was because God's mercy and grace was upon them in the same way it had been upon me. However, the people were so blinded that they couldn't see that Jesus was trying to help them. As Jesus looked at lost humanity, He wept. I noticed that nobody was trying to warn or help these people. That's when Jesus turned and looked at me.

Jesus allowed me to feel a small portion of what He feels for the lost. It was more than I could bear. My heart split from the pain it caused God. The only thing Jesus cared about was the condition of their souls, but it seemed as though no one else cared. No one was trying to help them to be free from the power of the devil.

The lost people had no idea of the battle that was taking place for their lives. Out of the corner of my eye, I saw a large void and then saw hell. I watched in horror as people dropped one by one into hell, lost forever. When one person fell into the dark void of hell, others were so blinded they didn't even notice. They didn't understand that they were about to stumble in as well. To ensure the plan of Satan was not thwarted, demons hovered over the people. It looked like an assembly line of lost souls going into eternity, forever separated from God.

Called to Ministry

I was silent as I watched in horror. I could have been one of those souls on the assembly line to hell if Jesus had not intervened. He looked at me and in a serious tone asked, "Would you help them, as I helped you?"

Jesus looked into my heart. I knew He was seeing things I didn't even know were there. I felt very uncomfortable. I wanted to hide but couldn't. He saw my motives and desires. He told me He had asked others in my situation to help, but they were too ashamed of their past and said no.

Jesus was very clear that it would be my choice. If I said no, I would still go to heaven and would be with Him forever. I could live a private life and not tell anyone about my background. He would allow me to have a very easy life if I wanted. He told me I could have what I really wanted, which was to have what I thought was a normal life and to be a housewife. However, He told me that if I said no, the people I saw would probably not make it to heaven because no one else was going to them. Jesus showed me that very few Christians witness. As a result, multitudes of people regularly drop into hell like clockwork. Jesus was very quiet as He turned to look at the lost people. "No one is telling them," He said. "Christians are allowing people to fall into hell just because they don't want to be bothered." There aren't words to describe the grief I saw in Jesus' heart.

I thought about what people would think about me and maybe even do to me if I said yes to what He was asking. I thought about the impact this would have on my family. I didn't want them to be embarrassed. I would have preferred to have a private life where I could hide rather than publicize what had happened to me. But I realized that I had to publicly share my background to warn people about hell and expose the deceptions of the devil.[6]

I knew if I said no, I couldn't live with myself. I knew I would be responsible for some of those people falling into hell because I could have warned them, but consciously chose not to for selfish reasons. When I looked at the images of the lost, I knew that picture would remain with me for the rest of my life. I would never be able to shake it from my memory. I thought about the price that Jesus paid so I wouldn't have to go to hell. How could I not spend the rest of my life warning people about the dangers of hell?

With tears in my eyes, I looked at the people and then at Jesus. "Of course, Lord," I whispered. I let go of the desires I had for my life and gave the remainder of my life to the Lord. I was committed to bringing the Gospel message to the lost. That day, I felt as though the dreams I had for my life died. However, I later learned that my decision is what truly gave me "a life."[7]

Jesus' Departure

At this point, Jesus had been with me for several days. The time came, however, when He told me He couldn't be with me in a manifested presence all of the time. I didn't understand what He was saying and begged Him to stay. He told me, "Go to church tonight. The minister there will help you." I had seen a particular church on TV and knew that the Lord was telling me to attend that church.

Jesus told me I needed to receive pastoral counseling so I would understand what happened to me. The church had a Bible school, and He instructed me to attend it as well. He was firm as He said a second time that He needed to go. He told me I knew His voice now and to follow His leading for the next steps I was to take. And just like that, I could no longer see Him.

I quickly went throughout my house, hoping I would still see Him. But I couldn't see Him anymore. However, I heard His voice just as clearly as if He were still there encouraging me. And I felt His presence. From this, I knew He was still with me but that His leading would be different now. He again told me to go to church that night so I would be ministered to.

After Jesus left, the demons came back to test me. I could see them and felt them striking at me. The feeling of wanting to die came back on me. I was terrified and didn't understand what was going on and wondered why this was happening to me. I cried out to Jesus and heard His voice inside of me say, "Go to church tonight." I didn't want to go to church in the condition I was now in but felt as though I didn't have any other option. I forced myself to follow His instructions.

Several hours later at the church service that night, when the minister got up to speak, he said, "Someone here has a spirit of suicide and violence." Although I was embarrassed because there were thousands of people in the sanctuary, I went forward. I was desperate. When I stood before the minister, he said, "Satan, leave this woman," and devils left me. I saw a bright light and felt a power like electricity go through my body. I collapsed to the floor and laid there for several moments. When I got up, altar care workers took me to a private room where they ministered to me.

I went home that night feeling better, but I was in a state of shock from everything that had happened. During the next several days, I could still feel devils lurking around me. They tried to torment me in their old familiar ways, but the degree of their torment was not as strong. It was more like a thick heaviness that surrounded me.

Pastoral Counseling

My mind reeled from all I was going through. I kept rehearsing another instruction from the Lord, which was to receive pastoral counseling so I could understand what was happening to me. I desperately wanted to talk to someone but was afraid of being rejected or laughed at. But, I went through with it. Clenching my fists, I called the church I had just gone to, and asked if I could receive pastoral counseling. Fortunately, the person I talked to responded to me as though this was a common request. I breathed a sigh of relief. She scheduled me for an appointment. I was very nervous as I went.

A soft spoken, professionally-dressed woman greeted me. She had very warm eyes. I felt a strong presence of the Lord as I entered her office, similar to how it was when I'd met Him. This made me relax somewhat. As we started talking, she seemed to be speaking with the Lord in the same way He'd been speaking with me. I studied her because I'd never met anyone like her before. She seemed to really know God and was filled with love and peace. This was what I wanted when I was a psychic, but never got.

I shared my story with her, bit by bit. She didn't judge or reject me. Instead, she believed me and was excited that I wanted to be a Christian. With each story I told her, she referenced her well-worn bible, showing me scriptures on what I had experienced. The bible was opening up a new world to me I never knew existed. She seemed to know that book inside and out. I had never seen anyone do that before. My counselor taught me how to hear God's voice in my own heart, by observing her do the same. She taught me that the voice of God always parallels the truth of bible. And, she said, *"If it doesn't, it is not from God."* She tenderly shared with me scriptures on who the devil is and how he counterfeits God. (This meeting began several months of counseling I received from that precious woman. I also quickly registered for my first of two bible schools.)

Repent?

As I started pastoral counseling, I heard the Lord's voice again. He gave me the final instruction I needed. He explained that to be a Christian I not only needed to believe in Him, I also needed to repent of being a sinner. However, from my New Age days, I remembered how my teachers and New Age pastor described sin as spiritual abuse. I had so much false training that sin wasn't real, and I no longer believed I was a sinner.

To teach me sin was real and that I was a sinner, Jesus brought back the memory from a few days earlier of seeing the demons that were assigned to me. He reminded me that my spirit guides were really demons. From this I saw, in black and white, that I had been serving Satan and not God. Jesus was uprooting my self-deception. I remembered His initial warning to me that New Age was darkness and how I'd directly rebelled against Him by becoming a psychic. The truth struck my heart. The pain of realizing what I had done and seeing the darkness of my own heart was too much for me. I knew I couldn't blame Satan for what happened to me. And, I couldn't blame my New Age teachers, either. I did it. Not only was sin real, but I had sinned. And if I had sinned, I was a sinner.

Even though Jesus showed me the truth, I was horrified at what I had done and didn't want to admit it to myself. I just couldn't look at what I had become through my own sin. It was the truth, and I knew it. I thought in dismay, *And what was going to happen to the students I taught?* I remembered seeing the lost dropping into hell, one by one. Then I thought of the faces of my former clients and students. *Would they go there?* This was even harder to face than the vision of hell because I was responsible.

I didn't push Jesus away, but I also didn't respond to Him. I sat in a stunned silence. Jesus didn't press me beyond this conversation but gave me time to think about it. He asked me to go to church Sunday and respond to the altar call for salvation and repent for being a sinner and for what I'd done as a psychic. Then, He said He would forgive everything I had done.[8]

Disobeying the Lord's Instruction to Repent

That Sunday I went to church. I hoped people wouldn't recognize me from having had demons cast out of me the previous Sunday. I held my head up and went into the service, ignoring glances from people. Throughout the service, all I could think about was Jesus telling me I had to repent. I broke out in a cold sweat when the minister gave the invitation. I was embarrassed at having to go forward. But instead of stepping out into the aisle, I sat frozen in my seat. The service ended shortly afterward, and I left the church knowing I had disobeyed the Lord.

Throughout the next weeks, I began attending church regularly—the entire time internally battling with my need to repent. At each service, the Lord continued dealing with me to go forward, and I continued to delay it. It wasn't as much about the altar call as it was honoring the Lord with the Bible's requirement of repentance. I wanted Jesus, but even more, I wanted to hide from myself.

I knew the Lord wasn't pleased with me as the weeks dragged into months. I wavered back and forth from what the Lord told me about my old New Age belief that sin wasn't real. And the more I reasoned with myself, the more I could justify yielding to the familiar self-deception I hid beneath for so many years.

God allowed me to disobey Him for months, but my disobedience cost me. As I delayed my repentance, my salvation was also delayed. Because of this, the demons could still come and go to torment me. Although I didn't yet understand these truths from the Bible, at the point of my salvation, the demons would lose their rights to me. I would no longer be in Satan's kingdom but would be safe and secure in God's kingdom. This is the only reason why the demons had a right to continue tormenting me, and they took full advantage of it. They mercilessly got their last jabs in at me during this time. All I had to do was repent, and Satan would lose access to me. But I chose to suffer the torments of Satan rather than face the truth and let God change me.

I justified that because I had an experience with Jesus and knew He was the son of God, I was saved based on my experience. And every time I sat through an altar call, I kept rationalizing that my experience was enough. I wanted to believe the New Age doctrine that I could elevate my spiritual experience above the truth of God's Word. That way I wouldn't have to face what I had done. I wanted to experience the beauty of Christianity without having to accept the personal responsibility of being a sinner. However, the truth is that every person alive has sinned and everyone has to come to the Lord the same way. And that is through simple faith in Jesus Christ and repentance from being a sinner. This is the crux of Christianity and no one can get around it, as I was about to find out.

As I sat through church services, I kept hearing scriptures preached from the pulpit that paralleled what Jesus was telling me. I couldn't get away from the fact that I had to believe in Jesus *and* repent.

I heard scriptures like: Acts 3:19, *"Repent ye therefore, and be converted, that your sins may be blotted out...."* I also heard Second Corinthians 7:9-11, *"... your sorrow led you to repentance ... Godly sorrow brings repentance that leads to salvation and leaves no regret, but worldly sorrow brings death. See what this godly sorrow has produced in you...."*

Repent means "to feel remorse or sorrow for" and "to turn away from." God requires you to repent for the spiritual condition of being a sinner. He doesn't require you to repent for every sin you've ever committed. If so, what if you forgot to repent of one sin? Then would your salvation be null and void? Of course not. God is a God of grace and forgiveness, and He looks at the motives of your heart. God only asked me to repent of the specific sin of witchcraft, in addition to asking me to repent of being a sinner, because in my heart I was refusing to recognize it as sin.

You don't need to respond to an altar call in order to be saved either. You can be saved publicly or privately. The Lord asked me to respond to an altar call to honor Him.

God allowed me to delay repentance for a time, but the day was quickly approaching when I would have to choose.[9]

---

[1]*"And immediately there fell from his eyes as it had been scales: and he received sight forthwith, and arose, and was baptized"* (Acts 9:18). *"In whom the god of this world hath blinded the minds of them which believe not, lest the light of the glorious gospel of Christ, who is the image of God, should shine unto them"* (2 Corinthians 4:4).

[2]*"Then thou scarest me with dreams, and terrifiest me through visions"* (Job 7:14). *"Moreover the word of the LORD came unto me, saying, Jeremiah, what seest thou? ...Then said the LORD unto me, Thou hast well seen..."* (Jeremiah 1:11-12).

[3]*"And from the wicked their light is withholden..."* (Job 38:15).

[4]*"And the Lord said unto Satan, Hast thou considered my servant Job, that there is none like him in the earth, a perfect and an upright man, one that feareth God, and escheweth evil?"* (Job 1:8).

[5]*"And having spoiled principalities and powers, he made a shew of them openly, triumphing over them in it"* (Colossians 2:15).

[6]"I shall not die, but live, and declare the works of the Lord." (Psalm 118:17). "But none of these things move me, neither count I my life dear unto myself, so that I might finish my course with joy, and the ministry, which I have received of the Lord Jesus, to testify the gospel of the grace of God" (Acts 20:24). "... therefore hear the word at My mouth and give them warning from Me. If I say to the wicked, You shall surely die, and you do not give him warning or speak to warn the wicked to turn from his wicked way, to save his life, the same wicked man shall die in his iniquity, but his blood will I require at your hand" (Ezekiel 3:17-18 AMP).

[7]"For whosoever will save his life shall lose it: and whosoever will lose his life for my sake shall find it" (Matthew 16:25). "But [his word] was in mine heart as a burning fire shut up in my bones..." (Jeremiah 20:9).

[8]"But where sin abounded, grace did much more abound..." (Romans 5:20).

[9]"... My spirit shall not always strive with man..." (Genesis 6:3). "... choose you this day whom ye will serve..." (Joshua 24:15).

Chapter 7

MY PRISON CELL IN HELL

"But God said unto him, Thou fool, this night thy soul shall be required of thee . . . ."

—Luke 12:20

One evening, I went to church when a guest minister was preaching. At the conclusion of his message, while he was giving an altar call for people to come forward to be saved or to rededicate their lives to the Lord, he had a word of knowledge. "There is someone here," He said, "who needs to repent of witchcraft." His words pierced my heart. My internal wrestling match had come to a head, as the preacher's words cut me to the core. I didn't want to get up and go to the altar in front of people who now knew me. I couldn't handle the embarrassment of my new Christian friends thinking I wasn't really born again.

I reasoned that this altar call was for salvation, so this word of knowledge couldn't possibly be for me. I thought *I'm saved. I believe in Jesus now.* However, I still had not repented and would not repent. No one in the church moved. "Someone here needs to repent of witchcraft," the guest minister said again. I looked down. I didn't want to go forward and continued reasoning with myself. *Surely, this is for someone else. I saw Jesus. He called me into ministry.* I had become a church member. I was even winning souls to Christ with the street evangelism team.[1] However, only I knew I hadn't repented for being a sinner or for being a psychic, as Jesus asked me to for months. The guest minister kept looking around. When no one responded, he shrugged his shoulders and moved on with the service. I was relieved that I was able to keep my dignity and believed all was well. Or so I thought.

Would My Pride Take Me to Hell?

After the service, I drove back to my house with a friend, and she came in to visit for a little while. We were talking about the service and that unusual altar call when I began to feel ill. I felt as though something grabbed me on the side of my head. The pain was so intense that I suddenly had to lie down on my living room floor. My friend tried to make me feel comfortable, but I began to throw up. The sensation of being grabbed intensified. It felt as though a claw was ripping through the side of my head—the exact place where Jesus had touched me to set me free. All of my strength left my body, and I felt as though I was going to pass out. I knew that a devil was physically attacking me and I was scared.

I didn't understand what was happening because I reasoned that Jesus had already set me free from the devil. I said to myself, "No demon had the right to attack me." However, I knew the demons were able to harass me because I never repented. Deep down, I knew I had an open door to the devil because I didn't follow Jesus' final instructions. The words of the preacher kept flooding through my mind, "Someone needs to repent. . . ." I kept telling myself I was truly saved. I kept trying to lie to myself, but I couldn't lie to God.

My friend became very concerned and began praying for me. The pressure in my head was excruciating. Inside my spirit, I heard the words, brain aneurism. It felt as though something had burst inside of my head.

Then, I began seeing into the spirit realm. (See graphic: Escort to Hell). I saw a creature that looked like the dragons I had seen in Chinese New Year celebrations. It had a large head with horns and spikes coming out of it. Its reptilian body was much larger than I was. And it had one of its claws on and in my head. I tried to fight against it, but it was much stronger and larger than I was. I was powerless against it. I knew this creature had been assigned to escort me to hell.[2]

My strength was fading and I felt as though I was about to lose consciousness. I willed myself to stay here on earth. I knew life was on earth. As I looked into the spirit realm, it was pitch black and devoid of all life. I was so afraid. I looked for Jesus but I couldn't see Him anywhere. Somehow in the darkness, I could see this large dragon-like demon in front of me. It was extremely angry and would throw its head back, snorting like a bull. I could feel the demon's rage and hatred for me. This beast had a singular focus as it crossed its place of darkness and reached into the realm of life that I was in. It was determined to take me to hell. And it had a right to.

Now, I was terrified. It seemed as though my spirit was separating from my body. I tried to scream from my physical body, but no sound would come out of my mouth. Although my physical body was lying still on the floor, another part of me—my spirit—was very much alive and fighting with all my strength. In the spirit realm, I screamed out to God, "I'm saved. Jesus, what is happening?" I crossed back and forth between the two realms. I kept looking back to my living room and tried with all of my might to stay in that realm. Then the demon would pull me further into the darkness. I desperately searched for Jesus as I tried to push against the demon.

I was desperate not to go to hell. In my spirit I screamed, "I'm a church member! I'm going to Bible school, just like you told me to. Oh God, please help me!" I heard no response.

When I would cross back into the physical realm, I was able to open my eyes and look at my friend. She was scared and was crying out to God for help. She did the only thing she knew to do, which was to read scriptures from the Bible. As she read aloud from the Word of God, the demon would let go of its grip on me. It couldn't stand hearing the Word. The demon couldn't touch my friend, but it could touch me. And it kept coming back for me. I was horrified. I would have done anything to go back to the church and respond to the altar call. But it was too late. My pride was taking me to hell!

A Prison Cell Awaited Me

At one point, when the demon took me further—but not completely—into the darkness, I saw my final destination in hell. I saw a prison cell that was reserved for me. I fought with all my strength to remain on the earth. Desperately, I looked around for help, but there was no one to help me. Jesus wasn't there. And I didn't see any living person in the pitch black darkness.

The prison cell was about 8 feet wide by 8 feet long and 8 feet high. The black steel bars were firmly fused into the cement floor.[3] The bars of the cell looked as though they had been burned many times. I looked up and saw a large ball of orange and red flames coming toward my cell. It would only be a matter of seconds before the cell and everything in it would be completely engulfed in fire. (See graphic: My Cell on Fire.) That demon was determined to lock me in that cell.

Although our physical bodies die, our spirit being does not. It lives forever. I was horrified when I realized that I would repeatedly experience being burned alive, yet never able to die.[4] I was so afraid.

My Torturers

About ten sinister looking demons were standing around the perimeter of the cell ready to torment me. They had been personally assigned to guard my cell. They were the color of pitch black. I had never seen a color of black as dark as these creatures were. They were pure evil and looked like professional executioners and torturers.[5] (See Graphic: My Torturers in Hell.)

When I crossed over into the spirit realm, I somehow knew things. I knew that these creatures had once been angels filled with God's light. But now, they were devoid of all light. When I realized this, I knew that my body would go through that same awful transformation if I wasn't able to hold on to my life on earth.

These demons looked at me with eagerness. They were full of self-satisfaction because another soul was entering their domain. Some demons held instruments with which to torture and inflict unimaginable pain on me. These instruments were unique to hell and were unlike anything I had ever seen. On earth, just a small amount of this kind of torture would have killed me. In hell, I would have to suffer through endless torture. I saw that my existence in hell would alternate between being burned alive and being mercilessly tortured.

The demons were not chained to one place, so they would move out of the way when the balls of fire passed through the prison cell.

As awful as what I was seeing was, I had the sense that the prison cell was only a holding place. I knew that something much worse was going to happen at some point. I knew these demons were getting their last jabs in before they were tormented as well. I prayed to God to save me.

Saved From Hell

Meanwhile, my friend called our church for help and was able to get through to a pastor. After she described what was happening to me, the pastor prayed and exercised his authority over the devil. Immediately, the pain in my head stopped. What felt like internal bleeding, suddenly stopped. The demon's claw that gripped my head was pried loose, and my spirit being was immediately sucked back into my body. When I opened my eyes and saw that I was back in my living room, I was shocked, relieved, and overwhelmed. I looked at my friend and began to cry. We were both shaken by what had just happened. In horror, I realized I had just been saved from hell.

After the shock of what happened wore off, when I was broken and alone, I finally repented to the Lord.[6] I asked God to forgive me. I finally allowed godly sorrow to flood my heart. I admitted that I was a sinner and that I was so sorry for what I had done. Surprisingly, the very moment I did, the Lord spoke to my heart and said that this simple repentance was all that He had wanted and required.

After I repented, I felt the intense grip of Satan leave me for good. I never again felt that hopeless prison I was locked in for so many years. Although I didn't yet understand the spiritual principles regarding the authority Christians have over the devil and that I just transferred from Satan's kingdom to God's kingdom,[7] I immediately experienced the effect. What was most surprising is that this event only took minutes. God didn't want me to stay in that place of repentance. He just wanted me to walk through it. As John 3:17 (NIV) says, *"For God did not send his Son into the world to condemn the world, but to save the world. . . ."*

Finally, I was saved! I felt God's love and mercy[8] surround me as I rested in the peace of His protection and salvation.

No one should experience the tortures of hell because God has already made a way of escape. Jesus said, *"I am the door: by me if any man enter in, he shall be saved"* (John 10:9). Salvation is a glorious, experience of surrender to Jesus Christ. If you have not accepted Jesus Christ as your Lord and Savior, I pray that you will receive God's gift of salvation. In Chapter 18 of this book, I outline simple instructions on how to give your life to the Lord.

---

[1] *"Not every one that saith unto me, Lord, Lord, shall enter into the kingdom of heaven; but he that doeth the will of my Father which is in heaven. Many will say to me in that day, Lord, Lord, have we not prophesied in thy name? and in thy name have cast out devils? and in thy name done many wonderful works? And then will I profess unto them, I never knew you: depart from me, ye that work iniquity"* (Matthew 7:21-23).

[2] *"Hell from beneath is moved for thee to meet thee at thy coming"* (Isaiah 14:9).

[3] *"And they shall be gathered together, as prisoners are gathered in the pit, and shall be shut up in the prison..."* (Isaiah 24:22).

[4] *"They shall be burnt with hunger, and devoured with burning heat, and with bitter destruction: I will also send the teeth of beasts upon them, with the poison of serpents of the dust"* (Deuteronomy 32:24).

[5] *"Yea, his soul draweth near unto the grave, and his life to the destroyers"* (Job 33:22). *"Yes, his soul draws near the Pit, And his life to the executioners"* (Job 33:22 NKJV). *"And his lord was wroth, and delivered him to the tormentors, till he should pay all that was due unto him* (Matthew 18:34). *"In anger his master turned him over to the jailers to be tortured..."* (Matthew 18:34 NIV)

[6] *"... and the mighty man shall be humbled..."* (Isaiah 5:15). *"... except ye repent, ye shall all likewise perish"* (Luke 13:3).

[7] *"Who hath delivered us from the power of darkness, and hath translated us into the kingdom of his dear Son"* (Colossians 1:13).

[8] *"Mercy and truth are met together; righteousness and peace have kissed each other"* (Psalm 85:10). *"Fear ye not, stand still, and see the salvation of the Lord, which he will shew to you to day: for the Egyptians whom ye have seen to day, ye shall see them again no more for ever. The Lord shall fight for you, and ye shall hold your peace"* (Exodus 14:13-14).

Surrendering to Jesus

Meeting My Demons

The Lost

Escort to Hell

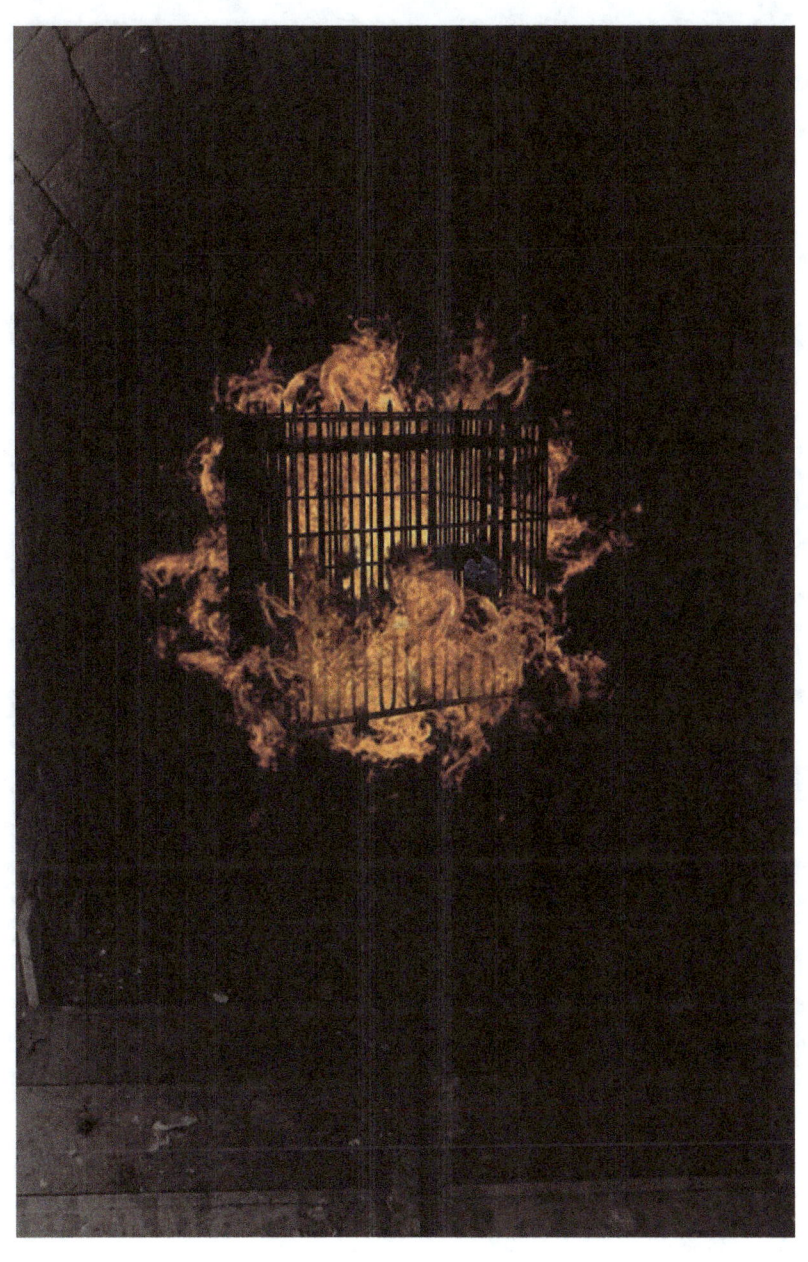

My Cell on Fire

Seeing Myself as a False Teacher

My Torturers in Hell

New Age

Chapter 8

COMPARING NEW AGE AND BIBLE DOCTRINE

The truth about New Age and the consequences of getting involved in it are hidden to most. But in First Corinthians 4:5, the Lord promises to *". . . bring to light the hidden things of darkness . . . ."* This chapter exposes the dangers of this growing belief system.

New Age is an eclectic group of philosophies and practices that were adapted from ancient and modern cultures. This belief system covers a broad range of beliefs that include reincarnation, holism, pantheism, and occultism, and health and wellness. New Age is typically viewed as metaphysical and paranormal. *Occult* is another term that is common for some New Age practices. The word *occult* means "hidden or concealed."

Let's examine New Age beliefs in comparison to Bible doctrine.

Everything Is God
vs.
God Exists; Man's Will Exists; and Satan Exists

This New Age doctrine believes that as long as you are active in some kind of spiritual search, then whatever that search is, it is God. It doesn't matter if you are taking a yoga class, learning Buddhist meditation, or developing your intuition or psychic abilities. I did all of these things, and all of my spiritual teachers said these activities were "of God." Even though something didn't feel right about them on the inside, everything looked right on the outside and sounded spiritual. So I kept taking class after class. You will see, however, from the following scriptures that the God of the Bible is the only true God and the only way to know God is through His son Jesus Christ.

> "I am the Lord: that is my name: and my glory will I not give to another..." (Isaiah 42:8).
>
> "I am the Lord, and there is none else, there is no God beside me..." (Isaiah 45:5).
>
> "...I am the Lord; and there is none else..." (Isaiah 45:18).
>
> "Verily, verily, I say unto you, He that entereth not by the door into the sheepfold, but climbeth up some other way, the same is a thief and a robber" (John 10:1).
>
> "Jesus saith unto him, I am the way, the truth, and the life: no man cometh unto the Father, but by me" (John 14:6).

This next belief is central to New Age thinking and is what hooks many people.

SINCE THERE IS SOME POWER, IT MUST BE OF GOD

vs.

THERE IS NO REAL POWER BUT THE POWER OF GOD

So often when people have a spiritual experience of any kind, they think it's from God. After I had gone to my first psychic reading, I remember thinking there is no way this wonderful spiritual experience couldn't be from God. *How else could this psychic have known those things about me?*

The strategy Satan uses in New Age is to counterfeit the power of the Holy Spirit as demonstrated in Christianity. God wants to demonstrate Himself in signs, wonders, and miracles. However, He does so within the boundaries of His Word, and His Word can never be broken. God wants you to yield yourself to Jesus Christ as the true God and allow Him to do the signs, wonders, and miracles. Outside of this protection, any supernatural activity is from the devil and is not safe.

Satan uses supernatural activity to trick people into following after this religion. Unsuspecting people think they are getting closer to God, but they are actually being drawn closer to hell. Because I experienced so much of the supernatural, I convinced myself that it had to be right, even though God Himself warned me against it.

Comparing New Age and Bible Doctrine

The following scriptures explain that false teachers exist and that they are not from God. The Bible terms these false teachers as "false prophets." As difficult as it was for me to admit when I was in New Age, I was one of these false prophets.

"And many false prophets shall rise, and shall deceive many" (Matthew 24:11).

". . . For false Christs and false prophets shall rise, and shall shew signs and wonders, to seduce, if it were possible, even the elect" (Mark 13:22).

"For such are false apostles, deceitful workers, transforming themselves into the apostles of Christ. And no marvel; for Satan himself is transformed into an angel of light. Therefore it is no great thing if his ministers also be transformed as the ministers of righteousness. . ." (2 Corinthians 11:13–15).

"But there were false prophets also among the people, even as there shall be false teachers among you, who privily shall bring in damnable heresies, even denying the Lord that bought them, and bring upon themselves swift destruction" (2 Peter 2:1).

"Beloved, believe not every spirit, but try the spirits whether they are of God: because many false prophets are gone out into the world. Hereby know ye the Spirit of God: Every spirit that confesseth that Jesus Christ is come in the flesh is of God: And every spirit that confesseth not that Jesus Christ is come in the flesh is not of God: and this is that spirit of antichrist. . ." (1 John 4:1–3).

From the above scriptures, the Bible outlines several facts about false prophets:

1) Many will exist

2) They will perform false signs

3) They can be identified because they deny Jesus Christ

Essentially, any supernatural power that a person "taps into" that is not from Jesus Christ is not of God but is from Satan. This was the hardest part of New Age for me to understand because I was having "real" experiences. New Age taught that everything was "God." I never believed that Satan was real or that it was Satan who was giving me counterfeit spiritual experiences.

This deception from hell tricked me into becoming a false prophet, and for a short time, I influenced people to follow after the devil instead of the true God. Satan's plan backfired, however. I am now more of a weapon *for* God because I have seen Satan's kingdom up close. I can easily expose Satan's deceptions and instead, influence people to go straight to heaven.

I know that God has completely forgiven me of my involvement in New Age, and He will completely forgive anyone who has fallen into this deception as well.

Below is a side-by-side comparison of seven basic New Age beliefs and seven basic Bible doctrines.

New Age Belief	Bible Doctrine
Everything is God; God is in everything.	God exists; Man's choice exists; and Satan exists.
Since there is some power, it must be of God. • To contact God, go to a medium. • If there are signs and wonders, it is from God	There is no real power except the power of God through Jesus. • To contact God, pray yourself, after you've been saved. • Not all signs and wonders are from God; Satan does false signs to deceive.
Spiritual search is inward to self. • With no consequence to sin, hell doesn't exist. • Your spiritual search will "save" and "heal" you. • You don't need a Savior.	Spiritual search is outward to God. • There are consequences to sin, and hell is very real. • You cannot "save" and "heal" yourself. • You need a Savior.
Spiritual search is lifelong.	Spiritual search is finally over.
Christianity is closed-minded and judgmental because it doesn't accept all religions.	Christianity opens up access to the one real God to all people through salvation.
Sin does not exist so there is no consequence to sin.	Sin does exist and there are consequences to sin.
Results of involvement: • Demonic oppression • Demonic possession • Eternity in hell	Results of involvement: • Wholeness • Deliverance • Eternity in heaven

Comparing New Age and Bible Doctrine

Counterfeit Techniques of the Devil

The following scripture outlines counterfeit techniques of the devil that God views as an abomination to Him.

> "When thou art come into the land which the Lord thy God giveth thee, thou shalt not learn to do after the abominations of those nations. There shall not be found among you any one that maketh his son or his daughter to pass through the fire, or that useth divination, or an observer of times, or an enchanter, or a witch. Or a charmer, or a consulter with familiar spirits, or a wizard, or a necromancer. For all that do these things are an abomination unto the Lord..." (Deuteronomy 18:9–12).

Every psychic I met said they wanted to "help" people. But you can see from the following verses that they can't help anybody.

> "... Let now the astrologers, the stargazers, the monthly prognosticators, stand up, and save thee from these things that shall come upon thee. Behold, they shall be as stubble; the fire shall burn them; they shall not deliver themselves from the power of the flame: there shall not be a coal to warm at, nor fire to sit before it. Thus shall they be unto thee with whom thou hast laboured, even thy merchants, from thy youth: they shall wander every one to his quarter; none shall save thee" (Isaiah 47:13–15).

I think the above verses are perfectly clear on how God views what is now called New Age. Reading these scriptures drove me to study the Bible on these topics. I had believed myself to be an intelligent, educated person who was genuinely helping people. But according to the Bible, the opposite was true. As I read the scriptures, I could no longer argue that what I believed in New Age was correct. And since I knew the Bible was true, all I could do was admit to myself the truth of how I had lived my life.

I think that is how sin is for many people, and it doesn't matter what the sin is. If you are caught up in sin, there is something inside of you that wants to hide from the truth and deceive yourself. But when your actions are held up to the Word of God, truth is exposed. You can either yield to the truth and let God transform you through His love, or you can hide from the truth and go further into darkness. Eventually, I chose to yield to the truth. In so doing, I studied more scriptures about New Age, specifically on the topic of psychics and mediums.

Contacting the Dead

One of the key beliefs of New Age is that we can contact deceased loved ones by going to a psychic or a medium. Many mediums communicate with what they believe are spirit guides, or angels. They believe that the spirit guides are helping them from "the other side." Today, psychics and mediums are being glamorized by prime time TV programs and movies. As a result, many people are falling prey to this device of Satan. One time I saw a commercial for a prime time television show that implied that mediums "saved souls" and to "not be afraid." It also made the audacious statement that "death was just the beginning."

The belief that you can communicate with deceased loved ones is very comforting to grieving families. But you have to realize this is a snare of the devil that uses grief to suck you into his trap. As I shared earlier, this is also what first hooked me. Here is what the Bible has to say about seeking psychics or mediums to contact the dead for you.

> "Regard not them that have familiar spirits, neither seek after wizards, to be defiled by them. . ." (Leviticus 19:31).
>
> "And the soul that turneth after such as have familiar spirits, and after wizards, to go a whoring after them, I will even set my face against that soul, and will cut him off from among his people" (Leviticus 20:6).
>
> "A man also or woman that hath a familiar spirit, or that is a wizard, shall surely be put to death: they shall stone them with stones: their blood shall be upon them" (Leviticus 20:27).
>
> "And he made his son pass through the fire, and observed times, and used enchantments, and dealt with familiar spirits and wizards: he wrought much wickedness in the sight of the Lord, to provoke him to anger" (2 Kings 21:6).
>
> "Moreover the workers with familiar spirits, and the wizards, and the images, and the idols, and all the abominations that were

spied in the land of Judah and in Jerusalem, did Josiah put away..." (2 Kings 23:24).

"And when they shall say unto you, Seek unto them that have familiar spirits, and unto wizards that peep, and that mutter: should not a people seek unto their God? for the living to the dead? ... if they speak not according to this word, it is because there is no light in them" (Isaiah 8:19–20).

"For they are the spirits of devils, working miracles, which go forth unto the kings of the earth and of the whole world..." (Revelations 16:4).

These scriptures are very clear about the dangers of going to mediums to contact deceased loved ones. Furthermore, there is no benefit to contacting a loved one who has passed on. Ecclesiastes 9:5 says *"... the dead know not anything."* And Job 7:9 points out that *"... he that goeth down to the grave shall come up no more."* This shows that the medium is *not* talking to your loved one. In reality, the medium is talking to a demon. When I had psychic readings to contact my sister, it was not my sister the psychic talked to—it was a demon.

Admitting the Truth

As I searched the Bible after my salvation experience, I had to face these scriptures. I had to admit that as a psychic, when I talked to my spirit guides or someone that had passed on, I was really talking to common devils. And absolutely no good came out it—for me or for others. God warns us about these practices in the Bible. We have to realize that He writes as a loving Father who doesn't want to see harm come to His children. Contrary to what some may believe, God isn't trying to keep spiritual experiences from His children. He just wants to make sure that what His children experience is from Him.

These truths were very hard for me to admit because everything "seemed" so real. I was having "real" spiritual experiences. In a New Age teaching I heard, the speaker stated that human beings were all meant to believe in something. He went on to say that once you had a legitimate experience with something, you no longer had to try to believe in it. You knew it was true because of the "experience." Looking back on this from a Christian perspective, it's easy to see Satan's trick is to reel people in with any kind of "experience." And once they have that "experience," he's got them.

This was how Satan tricked me. I had a spiritual experience and "felt" something. Although God tried to warn me on several occasions, I overrode those warnings. I believed a lie because of the experiences I had.

To get out from under this deception, I had to realize that Satan is a spiritual being. In fact, he was an angel that fell from God's presence through sin. He will always be a fallen spirit. When Satan fell, he deceived one third of the angels in heaven into following him. You need to realize that when you are involved in any New Age practices, you are opening yourself up to fallen angels. Of course, you are having "spiritual" experiences, but just because something is "spiritual" does not mean it has anything to do with God.

As I tried to understand what happened to me when Jesus saved me, I discovered many scriptures about "spiritual" experiences that were *not* from God. As I read about some of these experiences, I was amazed to see that they were essentially the same experiences I had. And if you are in New Age, you are probably having some of these experiences too.

SEPARATING REAL FROM FALSE

In the following verses, Moses was sent by God to deliver the Hebrews out of Pharaoh's slavery. God instructed Moses to perform certain signs in front of Pharaoh. You'll notice that Pharaoh's magicians were able to duplicate the signs through a counterfeit power from Satan. When the magicians threw their rods on the ground, their rods turned into snakes the same way Moses' rod did. However, Moses' snake ate the magician's snakes, demonstrating that God's power is much greater than Satan's.

> And Moses and Aaron went in unto Pharaoh, and they did so as the Lord had commanded: and Aaron cast down his rod before Pharaoh, and before his servants, and it became a serpent. Then Pharaoh also called the wise men and the sorcerers: now the magicians of Egypt, they also did in like manner with their enchantments. For they cast down every man his rod, and they became serpents: but Aaron's rod swallowed up their rods" (Exodus 7:10–12).

The second chapter of the book of Daniel records a time when King Nebuchadnezzar was distressed by a dream he had. He summoned his court magicians and astrologers to first tell him the dream he had and then interpret it for him. The magicians and astrologers were unable to do as the king commanded. The prophet Daniel was then summoned to interpret the dream. After Daniel interpreted the dream, he was honored by the king. The King recognized that God was with Daniel but not with the magicians. (See Daniel 2:1-47.)

This chapter in the book of Daniel is an excellent example of how the counterfeit powers that are used in New Age for divination and dream interpretation are limited and pale in comparison to the real supernatural power of God. In addition, we can see that God wants to bless His people with visions, wisdom, and dream interpretation. However, these things must be done God's way and for God's purposes. My eyes were opened to the lure of New Age when I realized that God wanted to share signs and wonders with His people when they seek Him with a right heart. I realized Satan had nothing to offer me with his counterfeit, and I wanted the real thing.

A similar incident happened in the book of Genesis. Pharaoh of Egypt had a dream that greatly troubled him. He sent for all of the magicians and wise men in Egypt to interpret the dream for him but none could. Although Joseph was in prison, he had a reputation for being able to interpret dreams, so he was brought before Pharaoh. Joseph was able to immediately interpret the dream, which ultimately saved Egypt and his family from a famine. (See Genesis 41:1-39.) This is another clear example that the power of the occult is powerless in comparison to the power of God.

The passages in the books of Genesis and Daniel show that there is a distinction between God's power and the devil's power. These verses show that the power of God is always greater.

The book of Acts records an incident where a sorcerer wanted access to the power of God without going through the door of salvation. The sorcerer tried to pay Peter for the power of God. Peter dismissed him saying:

> "Thy money perish with thee, because thou hast thought that the gift of God may be purchased with money. Thou hast neither part nor lot in this matter: for thy heart is not right in the sight of God. Repent therefore of this thy wickedness, and pray God, if perhaps the thought of thine heart may be forgiven thee. For I perceive that thou art in the gall of bitterness, and in the bond of iniquity" (Acts 8:20–23).

It's clear that God will not allow anyone to "use" His power for personal profit.

There's Nothing "New" in New Age

New Age is not new. It was around thousands of years before Christ. It is just an old sin that has been renamed and repackaged. A scripture that helped me understand the progression of the sin of self-deception is in Romans 1:25: *"Who changed the truth of God into a lie, and worshipped and served the creature more than the Creator, who is blessed forever."*

When I was a New Age teacher, I literally saw this scripture come to pass in my life. I was teaching a class on meditation. The purpose of this meditation was to bring the students higher spiritually. As we began the meditation portion of the class, my eyes were opened to the spirit realm, and I caught a glimpse of what I looked like to the one true God. (See graphic: Seeing Myself as a False Teacher).

As the Lord allowed me to see a glimpse into the spirit realm, I was gray and dead-looking, and I was in an area that was completely gray and immersed in darkness. This is exactly what the Lord warned me about before I became involved in New Age. A far distance from me was pure light, which I understood to be the kingdom of God. A great dark abyss separated the realm I was in from God's realm. I was trying to get to God, but because I was dark, I wasn't allowed. Each time I tried to climb higher spiritually, grotesque, dead-looking creatures grabbed me and pushed me back down. I physically felt this at the same time I was seeing it. The creatures hated me and were doing everything they could to keep me from crossing the chasm.

This experience only lasted a few moments. However, it frightened me so much that I stopped meditating and ended the class as quickly as I could appropriately do so. As a psychic, I knew I had the ability to contact the spirit realm through meditation. I saw how all of my spiritual activities could never get me across that dark abyss, and I realized that I was completely separated from God. Spiritually, I was dead, and it was an awful sight. There wasn't any life in anything I was doing. Although I didn't fully understand the Gospel message yet, I knew I was on the wrong track.

After I was born again, the Lord reminded me of this awful experience when I was leading a prayer group. As I prayed, He again opened my eyes. I saw the same picture but this time I saw how I looked to God as a Christian. I saw the effect of the power of salvation and how it had pulled me out of a dead, dark kingdom and brought me back to life. My spirit was now filled with light. I was securely in God's kingdom and on the opposite side of the chasm. The evil creatures were far from me and could not touch me again.

> "And besides all this, between us and you a great chasm has been fixed, so that those who want to go from here to you cannot, nor can anyone cross over from there to us" (Luke 16:26).

Chapter 9

SEARCHING FOR GOD

Inside of every man and woman is a void that can only be filled by God. But mankind's search to fill that void can take him in many directions. The next core belief of New Age is about that search:

SPIRITUAL SEARCH IS INWARD TO SELF

VS.

SPIRITUAL SEARCH IS OUTWARD TO GOD TO A SAVIOR

This belief in New Age teaches that a person needs to search inwardly for spiritual answers. And it is in complete contrast to the foundational belief of Christianity, which says that man is lost and cannot save himself and thus needs a Savior. When I sat in seminars and heard New Age teachings, this concept sounded so right. It is a subtle teaching that leads many people astray. The lie is this: If you can save yourself, why do you need a savior? Terminology that is used in this core belief is "inner healing," "learning to meditate to heal yourself," and "meditating to develop your spirituality."

When I was studying New Age, many instructors taught, "The belief that man is sinful is spiritually abusive." Even though as a child I was taught that Christ died on the Cross to redeem mankind from sin, I began to believe the New Age lie. It was comforting to me. When you took sin out of the equation, I could live any way I wanted to and not be convicted. I was able to be in charge of my own life and do whatever I pleased with no consequences. Sounds like a subtle form of pride and rebellion, doesn't it? Early in my New Age learning, I remember thinking, *This is great. I can sin and serve God too.*

People think they can ignore God's road signs of caution and warning without any type of bad consequences happening to them. That makes as much sense as trying to drive through a flooded road without being swept away by raging waters. No matter how much "mind over matter" and "positive thinking" is done, the driver will still experience life-threatening consequences.

The following scriptures show what the Bible says about people who ignore the principles of the Bible and do whatever they choose.

> *"There is a way which seemeth right unto a man, but the end there of are the ways of death"* (Proverbs 14:12).
>
> *"For there are many, of whom I have often told you and now tell you even with tears, who walk (live) as enemies of the cross of Christ (the Anointed One). They are doomed and their fate is eternal misery (perdition); their god is their stomach (their appetites, their sensuality) and they glory in their shame, siding with earthly things and being of their party"* (Philippians 3:18-19 AMP).

The following scriptures point out how mankind needs salvation, which is only available through Jesus Christ. Even though I took comfort in believing that I did not need to be convicted of sin, my entire life suffered as a result. Finally, I couldn't deny that the New Age beliefs were not right because of what I was experiencing.

> *"But the salvation of the righteous is of the Lord. . ."* (Psalm 37:39).
>
> *"I will take the cup of salvation, and call upon the name of the Lord"* (Psalm 116:13).
>
> *". . . Salvation is of the Lord"* (Jonah 2:9).
>
> *"And ye have not his word abiding in you: for whom he [God] hath sent, him [Jesus] ye believe not"* (John 5:38).
>
> *"For if ye live after the flesh, ye shall die: but if ye through the Spirit do mortify the deeds of the body, ye shall live"* (Romans 8:13).
>
> *"But we are bound to give thanks alway to God for you, brethren beloved of the Lord, because God hath from the beginning chosen you to salvation. . ."* (2 Thessalonians 2:13).

Spiritual Search Is Lifelong
vs.
The Spiritual Search Is Finally Over

New Age believes that since there is no specific salvation experience, spirituality is a lifelong search. And since there is no definite belief on the next life, your spiritual search is endless. I initially thought my spiritual search would be liberating; instead, it became maddening for me.

New Age does not have foundational or absolute truths. And because of this, I spent an enormous amount of money continually learning but never getting anywhere. I studied all of the major world religions because that seemed like a very spiritual thing to do. The more I studied, the more confused I became and the further I sank into depression.

However, when I surrendered my life to the Lord, I finally experienced an incredible peace that enveloped my entire being. None of the gods of the world's major religions were able to heal me of any disease or depression. Jesus was the only one who ever did; and His results were lasting. And when you experience the salvation that God provided through His Son Jesus Christ, you will have an assurance of your eternal destiny. The following scriptures show that you can have complete assurance that you will spend an eternity in heaven when you give your life to the Lord.

> "All that the Father giveth me shall come to me; and him that cometh to me I will in no wise cast out" (John 6:37).
>
> "And I give them eternal life, and they shall never lose it or perish throughout the ages. [To all eternity they shall never by any means be destroyed.] And no one is able to snatch them out of My hand. My Father, Who has given them to Me, is greater and mightier than all [else]; and no one is able to snatch [them] out of the Father's hand" (John 10:28–29 AMP).
>
> "Jesus answered, 'I told you, but you don't believe. Everything I have done has been authorized by my Father, actions that speak louder than words. You don't believe because you're not my sheep.

> My sheep recognize my voice. I know them, and they follow me. I give them real and eternal life. They are protected from the Destroyer for good. No one can steal them from out of my hand. The Father who put them under my care is so much greater than the Destroyer and Thief. No one could ever get them away from him. I and the Father are one heart and mind' " (John 10:28–29 Message).

> "He went once for all into the [Holy of] Holies [of heaven], not by virtue of the blood of goats and calves [by which to make reconciliation between God and man], but His own blood, having found and secured a complete redemption (an everlasting release for us)" (Hebrews 9:12 AMP).

Christianity Is Closed-Minded to Other Religions
vs.
Christianity Opens Up Access to the One Real God

New Age believes that Christians are judgmental because they are closed-minded to other religions. A fundamental New Age concept is that all roads lead to one God. Here is a snapshot of how Satan makes this particular deception seem true.

1. You are a good person on a spiritual search.
2. Because you are a good person on a spiritual search, everyone else on a spiritual search is a good person too.
3. Since there are no absolutes—no hell and no concept of sin—who knows who is really right and who is really wrong.
4. Because there are no absolutes, to condemn anyone from being on their "path" would be judgmental and wrong.
5. So just keep "searching."

One day when working as a psychic, I asked my spirit guide, "What is the purpose of this life?" The spirit guide answered, "To determine where you will end up in the next life."

If that doesn't send a chill down your spine, it certainly should. When you realize that spirit guides are simply common devils whose only purpose is to take you to hell, you can understand the dangers of New Age. These false truths are effectively hidden under the concept of being spiritually open. The conversation I had with that devil perfectly summarizes First Timothy 4:1, *"Now the Spirit speaketh expressly, that in the latter times some shall depart from the faith, giving heed to seducing spirits, and doctrines of devils."*

The correct way to understand the Christian perspective is always through the window of love. The Lord explained it to me this way: I should think of Him as though He were my spouse. Then I should think of all other religions as men who were not my spouse. The Lord asked me, "How do you think I would feel if you were married to me, but were also with them? Would that be closed-minded? Or is that pure love wanting to protect his wife?" I got the point. I saw how hurt the Lord is when mankind, whom He dearly loves, is deceived by believing other religions or strays from Him to follow another religion.

Here is another way to look at it. If there was only one God, wouldn't it make sense for Satan to try and confuse people by developing many religions? How would anyone know which religion and god was right? Satan attempts to make it look as though Christianity is judgmental by being closed-minded to other religions. And in doing so, it appears that Jesus is the one who is hurting people. And that breaks God's heart.

Below are scriptures that clearly show that *all* people are equally in need of salvation. You'll also see that God doesn't have favorites but loves and accepts everyone.

> *"For all have sinned, and come short of the glory of God"* (Romans 3:23).
>
> *"I am the door: by me if any man enter in, he shall be saved. . ."* (John 10:9).
>
> *"All that the Father giveth me shall come to me; and him that cometh to me I will in no wise cast out"* (John 6:37).
>
> *"For I know the thoughts and plans that I have for you, says the Lord, thoughts and plans for welfare and peace and not for evil, to give you hope in your final outcome. Then you will call upon Me, and you will come and pray to Me, and I will hear and heed you. Then you will seek Me, inquire for, and require Me [as a vital necessity] and find Me when you search for Me with all your heart.*

I will be found by you, says the Lord, and I will release you from captivity. . ." (Jeremiah 29:11-14 AMP).

"Yea, if thou criest after knowledge, and liftest up thy voice for understanding; If thou seekest her as silver, and searchest for her as for hid treasures; Then shalt thou understand the fear of the Lord, and find the knowledge of God" (Proverbs 2:3-5).

"And it shall come to pass, that whosoever shall call on the name of the Lord shall be saved" (Acts 2:21).

SIN DOESN'T EXIST, SO THERE IS NO CONSEQUENCE TO SIN
vs.
SIN DOES EXIST, AND THERE IS CONSEQUENCE TO SIN

New Age teaches that there is no sin. This is based on the fact that in New Age that there are no absolutes. And with no absolutes, anything goes. This philosophy is in complete contrast to the Bible, which states that because of the fall of man in the Garden of Eden, mankind is stuck in a fallen state. And without redemption, man will be lost eternally (John 3:16-17). The following scriptures further show that there are consequences to sin but God has made a way through His Son Jesus Christ to be redeemed from sin.

"And this is the condemnation, that light is come into the world, and men loved darkness rather than light, because their deeds were evil" (John 3:19).

"God gave them over in the sinful desires of their hearts to sexual impurity for the degrading of their bodies with one another. They exchanged the truth of God for a lie, and worshiped and served created things rather than the Creator—who is forever praised. Amen. Because of this, God gave them over to shameful lusts . . . Furthermore, since they did not think it worthwhile to retain the knowledge of God, he gave them over to a depraved mind, to do what ought not to be done. They have become filled with every kind of wickedness, evil, greed and depravity. They are full of envy, murder, strife, deceit and malice. They are gossips, slanderers, God-haters, insolent, arrogant and boastful; they invent ways of doing evil; they disobey their parents; they are senseless, faithless, heartless, ruthless. Although they know God's righteous decree that

those who do such things deserve death, they not only continue to do these very things but also approve of those who practice them" (Romans 1:24–32 NIV).

"For the wages of sin is death; but the gift of God is eternal life through Jesus Christ our Lord" (Romans 6:23).

"Even when we were dead in sins, hath quickened us together with Christ. . ." (Ephesians 2:5).

". . . taking vengeance on them that know not God, and that obey not the gospel of our Lord Jesus Christ who shall be punished with everlasting destruction from the presence of the Lord, and from the glory of his power" (2 Thessalonians 1:8–9).

RESULTS OF INVOLVEMENT IN NEW AGE
vs.
RESULTS OF INVOLVEMENT IN CHRISTIANITY

The final basic belief of New Age highlights the results of being involved in New Age or Christianity. Deuteronomy 28:14–15 shows you that if you *"go after other gods to serve them,"* curses will come upon you. When I became involved in New Age, I felt the effect of these curses, even though I never knew this warning existed in the Bible. Unfortunately, my ignorance did not remove the effect of disobedience to God's Word. The good news is that whenever you repent and follow after the Lord, the curses are removed. In my own life, I immediately began feeling the effect of being spiritually blessed when I got saved.

The 28th chapter of Deuteronomy lists both blessings and curses: blessings for those who follow after the Lord and curses for those who don't. Here is a list of the different ways you can be cursed for not following after God:

- You will be cursed in the city and in the country (v. 16).
- Your basket and bread bowl will be cursed (v. 17).
- Your children will be cursed (v. 18).
- Wherever you go and whatever you do will be cursed (v. 19).
- You will experience confusion and frustration in everything you do (v. 20).

- You will be afflicted with all types of diseases (vv. 21–24).
- You will be defeated by your enemies (v 25).
- Boils, tumors, scurvy, itch, madness, blindness, and panic are only a few of the diseases that will come upon you (vv. 27–28).

This next verse shows that curses don't come on a person without a reason.

> "... the curse causeless shall not come" (Proverbs 26:2).

The next passage of scripture shows that one of the consequences of opening up to New Age can be demon possession. And this is still a possible outcome in New Age today. Any part of New Age is dangerous. Please do not get involved with it! As a result of my activities, I became demon possessed and needed to be delivered.

> "And it came to pass, as we went to prayer, a certain damsel possessed with a spirit of divination met us, which brought her masters much gain by soothsaying . . . But Paul . . . said to the spirit, I command thee in the name of Jesus Christ to come out of her. And he came out the same hour" (Acts 16:16–18).

There are consequences for rejecting the Bible and there are consequences for receiving Christ as your Savior. In my case, I received deliverance from demonic torments as a result of being saved. I can never again deny that Jesus Christ is the only way to God. I had prayed to other gods, spent thousands of dollars studying other religions, and all I got in return was demon possession. I prayed one prayer to Jesus—free of charge—and He set me on the path to complete healing and freedom. Colossians 1:13 became a reality in my life. "[Jesus] *hath delivered* [me] *from the power of darkness, and hath translated* [me] *into the kingdom of his dear Son."*

As you can see from both scripture and my personal experience, the undeniable result of being involved in New Age is being tormented by the devil. And the undeniable result of surrendering your life to Jesus Christ is freedom and wholeness.

Satan and Demons

Chapter 10

LIBERTY TO THE CAPTIVES

> "The Spirit of the Lord GOD is upon me; because the LORD hath anointed me to preach good tidings unto the meek; he hath sent me to bind up the brokenhearted, to proclaim liberty to the captives, and the opening of the prison to them that are bound ..."
> —Isaiah 61:1

Through my childhood and New Age experiences, I came in direct contact with the power of the devil. I have learned the importance of understanding that there is an enemy, as well as understanding the authority Christians have over the devil.

The heart of God is for all of His children to live victorious lives, free from the hurts of the devil. The reason Jesus went to the Cross and allowed Himself to be crucified was to buy back all of mankind from Satan's control and abuse. However, Christians have to know that they've been set free from the devil in order to fully live in that freedom.

This chapter defines who Satan is and what demons are. Plus, you will learn how to be set free, as well as how to set others free.

WHO IS SATAN AND WHO ARE DEMONS?

Many names exist for the devil. The Bible records more than 40 names for this enemy of God. Some of them include

- Satan
- Lucifer
- Belial
- god of this world
- angel of light
- prince of this world

- Beelzebub
- adversary
- dragon
- serpent
- prince of devils
- power of the air
- wicked one

Satan is the leader of the demonic kingdom and devils, or demons, report to him. You will notice that I use the term "the devil" and "Satan" interchangeably. To understand who the devil and demons are, you need to understand where they came from.

Satan was originally an archangel whose name was Lucifer. He was called "the anointed cherub who covereth" (Ezek. 28:14). At one time, he had a central position in God's kingdom. He had many responsibilities, one of which was to worship at God's throne.

> "Thou hast been in Eden the garden of God; every precious stone was thy covering, the sardius, topaz, and the diamond, the beryl, the onyx, and the jasper, the sapphire, the emerald, and the carbuncle, and gold: the workmanship of thy tabrets and of thy pipes was prepared in thee in the day that thou wast created. Thou art the anointed cherub that covereth; and I have set thee so: thou wast upon the holy mountain of God; thou hast walked up and down in the midst of the stones of fire" (Ezekiel 28:13–14).

Lucifer was lifted up in pride because of His great beauty. He wanted to become like God and tried to exalt his throne above God.

> "Thou wast perfect in thy ways from the day that thou wast created, till iniquity was found in thee . . . Thine heart was lifted up because of thy beauty, thou hast corrupted thy wisdom by reason of thy brightness: I will cast thee to the ground, I will lay thee before kings, that they may behold thee" (Ezekiel 28:15–17).

This adversary of God incited a rebellion in heaven and deceived one third of the angels into joining his ranks.

> "And there was war in heaven: Michael and his angels fought against the dragon; and the dragon fought and his angels, And prevailed not; neither was their place found any more in heaven. And the great dragon was cast out, that old serpent, called the Devil, and Satan, which deceiveth the whole world: he was cast out into the earth, and his angels were cast out with him" (Revelation 12:7-9).

When the devil tried to battle against God, he was cast to the earth.

> "How art thou fallen from heaven, O Lucifer, son of the morning! How art thou cut down to the ground, which didst weaken the nations" (Isaiah 14:12).

> "And [Jesus] said unto them, 'I beheld Satan as lightning fall from heaven'" (Luke 10:18).

In their fallen state, demons are organized into several ranks. Ephesians 6:12 says that "... we wrestle not against flesh and blood, but against...

1) principalities,
2) against powers,
3) against the rulers of the darkness of this world,
4) against spiritual wickedness in high places."

In understanding who the devil and demons are, it is helpful to understand their nature. The following scriptures highlight the nature of the devil and demons. You can see that they are deceivers, thieves, tormentors, and that Satan is the god of this world.

Deceivers

> "For many deceivers are entered into the world, who confess not that Jesus Christ is come in the flesh. This is a deceiver and an antichrist" (2 John 1:7).

> "And the great dragon was cast out, that old serpent, called the Devil, and Satan, which deceiveth the whole world..." (Revelation 12:9).

THIEVES

"The thief cometh not, but for to steal, and to kill, and to destroy..." (John 10:10).

TORMENTERS

"And to them it was given that they should not kill them, but that they should be tormented five months: and their torment was as the torment of a scorpion, when he striketh a man" (Revelation 9:5).

GOD OF THIS WORLD

"In whom the god of this world hath blinded the minds of them which believe not..." (2 Corinthians 4:4).

WHERE DEMONS ARE LOCATED

According to Second Corinthians 12:2, three heavenly realms exist:

"I knew a man in Christ above fourteen years ago, (whether in the body, I cannot tell; or whether out of the body, I cannot tell: God knoweth;) such an one caught up to the third heaven."

The third heaven that Apostle Paul is describing is where God's throne is located. The second heaven is the current abode of Satan and his demons, as can be interpreted from Ephesians 2:2, where Satan is described as "the prince of the power of the air." Demons—or what Scripture refers to as spiritual wickedness—are located in "high places" as recorded in Ephesians 6:12. The first heaven is the actual atmosphere of the earth.

John 10:10 says, "The thief cometh not but to kill, steal, and destroy...." You only have to look around you to see the effects of the demons that are at work on the earth. The following scriptures describe some fallen angels imprisoned in hell, awaiting their final judgment:

> "... God spared not the angels that sinned, but cast them down to hell, and delivered them into chains of darkness, to be reserved unto judgment" (2 Peter 2:24).
>
> "And the angels who kept not their first estate, he hath reserved in everlasting chains under darkness unto the judgment of the great day" (Jude 1:6).

At the final judgment of God, the devil, demons, and fallen mankind—those who have not made Jesus Christ Lord of their lives—will then be cast into the Lake of Fire as their final location:

> "... and fire came down from God out of heaven, and devoured them. And the devil that deceived them was cast into the lake of fire and brimstone, where the beast and the false prophet are, and shall be tormented day and night for ever and ever" (Revelation 20:9–10).

THE DEVIL'S GOAL

Satan's goal is to deceive mankind into turning away from God's gift of salvation. The devil is destined to an eternity in hell, and he ultimately wants to take as many people with him as he can. The following scriptures point out Satan's objective:

> "Be sober, be vigilant; because your adversary the devil, as a roaring lion, walked about, seeking whom he may devour" (1 Peter 5:8).
>
> "And the Lord said, Simon, Simon, behold, Satan hath desired to have you, that he may sift you as wheat" (Luke 22:31).

Even though this is Satan's desire, he is limited by the laws of God. Christians who have surrendered their lives to Christ are under God's protection. Christians who know who they are in Christ and know that they are seated with Christ in heavenly places (Eph. 2:6), reign victoriously over the devil in this life. The devil is not victorious over Christians who know the Word of God and their authority in Christ. Because of this, Christians can enjoy a peace that the rest of the world cannot. No matter what comes their way, they can overcome.

Chapter 11

HOW DEMONS TORMENT PEOPLE

Prior to understanding how demons torment people, it is necessary to first know how God created mankind. When you understand how you were created, you can better understand the different ways the devil is able to torment you. Man is made up of three parts. He has a spirit, soul, and body. Your spirit is the real you. And your soul is made up of your mind, will, and emotions. The following scripture shows the three parts of man:

> "... I pray God your whole spirit and soul and body be preserved blameless unto the coming of our Lord Jesus Christ" (1 Thessalonians 5:23).

From this scripture, you can see that the soul of man is different than the spirit of man:

> "For the word of God is... sharper than any two-edged sword, piercing even to the dividing asunder of soul and spirit..." (Hebrews 4:12).

During salvation, the spirit of man is what is recreated. It is made alive and becomes completely new. Second Corinthians 5:17 states that a born again Christian is "... *a new creature: old things are passed away; behold, all things are become new.*" The soul of man remains in a fallen nature and must be "renewed." Christians are told to, "... *receive with meekness the engrafted word, which is able to save your souls*" (James 1:21). This is done by reading and meditating on scriptures in the Bible.

When you understand that man is comprised of three parts, it is easier to understand that the devil can torment people in three different ways. In the simplest form of torment, people can be influenced by or simply yield to demonic spirits. An example of this would be a person who yields to anger instead of remaining calm. In other instances, someone may allow fear to dominate him instead of trusting that God will take care of him.

The two primary ways that people can be tormented by demons are through oppression and possession. Oppression is a lesser affliction where Satan has a hold on a person's life in their body or soul, which is the mind, will, and emotions. Possession is a greater affliction where Satan has gained a partial or complete hold on a person's life, even by occupying their spirit.

Demons can afflict people in oppression and possession in varying degrees. When I was a child, at times, it felt as though a darkness would settle upon me. I was being oppressed by the devil. This oppression was so severe that I constantly thought about committing suicide. Other people may experience a similar oppression but not to the point where they want to take their life.

The devil usually begins to oppress people in their minds. He does this through thoughts. We are told in Second Corinthians 10:5 to cast "... *down arguments and every high thing that exalts itself against the knowledge of God, bringing every thought into captivity to the obedience of Christ.*" You may have thoughts of jealousy or fear enter your mind. If those thoughts are not cast down, oppression can result.

Another example of oppression can be an unsaved person struggling with lust. Someone may inadvertently click on a Web site that has pornography on it. Most people will quickly get off of the Web site. But a thought goes through the person's mind, *One quick look won't hurt.* The individual has the opportunity to cast that thought down and get off the Web site or give in to the thought. Let's say the person gives in to the thought. He looked once, then twice, and before he knew it, he was visiting the site every day. As the person continues to yield to the spirit, he can eventually become possessed by a spirit of lust. At that point, he does not want to be delivered from pornography.

Demons can torment non-Christians by entering any or all of the three parts of their being: their body, soul, or spirit. However, it is important to point out that Christians cannot be possessed in their spirit. After I repented and was finally was saved, I experienced Satan's grip pulled from me for good. This was my spirit being delivered as I was transferred from Satan's kingdom to God's kingdom. As I described earlier, I didn't understand the spiritual principles of what was happening to me, but I immediately felt the effect. Born-again Christians have been rescued "*. . . from the kingdom of darkness transferred into the kingdom of God's dear Son*" (Col. 1:13 NLT). It is impossible for a born-again Christian to belong to both kingdoms at the same time.

As a Christian, I was no longer possessed in my spirit, but for a time, I still was oppressed in my soul. The complete deliverance in my soul transpired over a period of years. I attended several Bible schools and studied the truth of God's Word. The more of God's Word that I got into my heart, the more the devil's hold on me was pried loose and I was set free from remaining oppression.

BIBLICAL EXAMPLES OF DEMONIC POSSESSION

The Bible gives examples of demon oppression and possession in the form of:

1) oppression of the physical body,

2) oppression of the mind,

3) partial possession, and

4) full demonic possession.

You will also see that:

1) both adults and children are tormented by demons,

2) varying degrees of possession and oppression exist in the body, soul and/or spirit, and

3) the presence of sin as the cause of possession or oppression is not always indicated in Scripture.

From the following biblical examples, you will see that in some instances, sin gave entrance to demonic activity. In other cases, there is no indication of how the person became oppressed or possessed. Scripture also shows that both children and adults can become demon oppressed or possessed.

The following verse shows that Jesus healed people who were oppressed in their bodies and minds, as well as people who were demon possessed.

> "... and they brought unto [Jesus] all sick people that were taken with divers diseases and torments, and those which were possessed with devils, and those which were lunatick, and those that had the palsy; and he healed them" (Matthew 4:24).

This next example is an adult who had a physical illness that was caused by what the Bible calls a "spirit of infirmity." These verses do not indicate how the woman became oppressed by the devil. But regardless of how the devil got there or the length of time the woman suffered, Jesus was able to set her free.

> "And, behold, there was a woman which had a spirit of infirmity eighteen years, ... And when Jesus saw her, he ... said unto her, Woman, thou art loosed from thine infirmity. And he laid his hands on her: and immediately she was made straight, and glorified God" (Luke 13:11–13).

ATTACKING YOUNG CHILDREN

Next, is an example of a young boy who became demon possessed. The passage does not indicate if sin was the cause of the child's possession. Although the young boy was helpless to free himself from demonic bondage, the desperate and loving care of his father enabled the young child to come in contact with the Deliverer, Jesus Christ.

> "And he asked his father, How long is it ago since this came unto him? And he said, Of a child. And ofttimes it hath cast him into the fire, and into the waters, to destroy him ... When Jesus saw that the

people came running together, he rebuked the foul spirit, saying unto him, Thou dumb and deaf spirit, I charge thee, come out of him, and enter no more into him. And the spirit cried, and rent him sore, and came out of him. . ." (Mark 9:21-22; 25-26).

The Bible also records an incident where a woman's young daughter was afflicted by a demon. Although it is not clear, it appears the young child was mentally tormented rather than physically tormented. When I examine these verses, I believe the young girl was possessed and not oppressed. Either way, Jesus addresses the girl's problem and sets her free.

"And, behold, a woman of Canaan . . . cried unto him, saying, Have mercy on me, O Lord, thou son of David; my daughter is grievously vexed with a devil. But he answered her not a word. And his disciples came and besought him, saying, Send her away; for she crieth after us. But he answered and said, I am not sent but unto the lost sheep of the house of Israel. Then came she and worshipped him, saying, Lord, help me. But he answered and said, It is not meet to take the children's bread, and to cast it to dogs. And she said, Truth, Lord: yet the dogs eat of the crumbs which fall from their masters' table. Then Jesus answered and said unto her, O woman, great is thy faith: be it unto thee even as thou wilt. And her daughter was made whole from that very hour" (Matthew 15:22-28).

These two examples impacted me greatly because they clearly show how innocent children can be afflicted by the devil, as I had been. And both examples show how Jesus restored these children.

Demonic Possession

The book of Mark records an example of full demonic possession in an adult. This is the story of the man from Gadara who was possessed in his spirit, soul, and body. In full demon possession, the afflicted person no longer has control of him or herself. In other words, the devil completely controls the person's behavior and life. This man from Gadara had supernatural strength beyond what any normal person could have, showing demonic power was present.

Before Jesus set this man free from the power of the devil, the demons identified themselves as Legion. Scripture shows the severity of the man's demon possession. The name "Legion" indicates the number of demons that inhabited the man. A Roman legion was comprised of 2,000 to 5,000 soldiers. I believe the reason Jesus asked, *"What is your name?"* in Mark 5:9 was to highlight the presence of many demons and show the dramatic deliverance. In doing so, a beautiful story of an extreme deliverance is shown.

What is most compelling to me in this story is the compassion that Jesus showed towards this individual man. When Jesus and His disciples set sail to the region of Gadara, He and his disciples encountered a fierce storm as they crossed the lake. But once they reached Gennesaret, Jesus only ministered to this one man before leaving the region again. This story is a great example of the lengths that the Lord will go through to reach one person. From that, we see how important each person is to God, no matter the condition they are in. And the effect of delivering the demon-possessed man was far reaching, for himself and the entire region. The man ended up evangelizing his entire city and region with his testimony. (See Mark 4:35–41; 5:1–20.)

SIN OPENS THE DOOR

The following examples show that sin was the cause of demon possession. Witchcraft is sin, and being involved in any type of witchcraft can open you up to demon possession. It is interesting to note that the young girl afflicted in this passage was possessed by a spirit of divination that correctly identified Paul and Silas as "servants of the most high God." However, Paul was able to discern that these statements were demonically inspired.

> *". . . a certain damsel possessed with a spirit of divination met us, . . . The same followed Paul and us, and cried, saying, These men are the servants of the most high God, which shew unto us the way of salvation. And this did she many days. But Paul, being grieved, turned and said to the spirit, I command thee in the name of Jesus Christ to come out of her. And he came out the same hour"* (Acts 16:16–18).

It is commonly believed that Mary Magdalene was the woman who was caught in adultery and brought to Jesus. (See John 8:3–11.) The following scriptures about Mary Magdalene record that she had seven demons cast out of her. It is thought that she opened herself up to demon possession through sexual sin, although the scripture is not clear.

> "And certain women, which had been healed of evil spirits and infirmities, Mary called Magdalene, out of whom went seven devils" (Luke 8:2).

Mary Magdalene's story is fascinating. Her life was dramatically changed after her encounter with Jesus. After Jesus rose from the dead, Mary was the first person He appeared to. Essentially, Mary became the first female evangelist in the Bible! She told the other disciples that she saw the resurrected Christ.

> "Now when Jesus was risen early the first day of the week, he appeared first to Mary Magdalene, out of whom he had cast seven devils. And she went and told them that had been with him, as they mourned and wept" (Mark 16:9–10).

This is a wonderful example of how being delivered from demons can transform a person's life. Just because someone needs demons to be cast out of them, doesn't mean that their life is over or that they will be permanently flawed because demons were once present. They can be set completely free from the power of the devil and bring glory to God for the rest of their lives.

Chapter 12

CASTING OUT DEVILS

I believe it is best to keep things simple. God makes things simple while Satan complicates things. The devil does this to confuse people so they won't do anything, especially when it comes to casting out devils. Whoever I minister to and however they became oppressed or possessed—I simply cast the devil out in Jesus' name. That is as complicated as it needs to be.

Many people try to figure out if the person is oppressed or possessed, how they opened the door to the devil, and what sins they need to repent of. Ministering deliverance is not that complicated. Demons know that all a Christian has to do is use the name of Jesus and they have to leave. The only times I've had success in ministering deliverance is when I've stuck to the simplicity of using Jesus' name and standing strong in the knowledge of my authority over Satan. And I recommend you to do the same.

The previous chapter covered several examples of Jesus casting out demons. We will now look at five principles that were a part of Jesus' deliverance ministry.

1. Casting Out Demons Was a Part of Jesus' Ministry

Jesus did not identify deliverance as His entire ministry. However, it was an integral part of His ministry. Because Jesus is our example to follow, Christians should not focus their ministry solely on deliverance. It is a valid component of ministry, but it should not be an isolated ministry.

After Jesus had been tempted in the wilderness, He returned to Galilee and began teaching in the synagogues. When God first launched Jesus into ministry, He went to a synagogue in Nazareth and began reading from Isaiah 61. Jesus' purpose in quoting this scripture was twofold: First, to identify Himself to the religious leaders that He was the Messiah; and second, to define His ministry. From the verses of scripture Jesus read, He outlined the various components of His ministry.

> *"The Spirit of the Lord is upon me, because he hath anointed me to preach the gospel to the poor; he hath sent me to heal the brokenhearted, to preach deliverance to the captives, and recovering of sight to the blind, to set at liberty them that are bruised"* (Luke 4:18).

Jesus went on to say, *"This day is this scripture fulfilled in your ears"* (Luke 4:21). Not long after Jesus proclaimed who He was, He had an opportunity to cast the devil out of a man.

> *"And in the synagogue there was a man, which had a spirit of an unclean devil, and cried out with a loud voice, Saying, Let us alone; what have we to do with thee, thou Jesus of Nazareth? art thou come to destroy us? I know thee who thou art; the Holy One of God. And Jesus rebuked him, saying, Hold thy peace, and come out of him. And when the devil had thrown him in the midst, he came out of him, and hurt him not"* (Luke 4:33–35).

Here is another scripture that reinforces that Jesus' ministry included casting out devils.

> *"How God anointed Jesus of Nazareth with the Holy Ghost and with power: who went about doing good, and healing all that were oppressed of the devil; for God was with him. . ."* (Acts 10:38).

2. Jesus Had Compassion on the Afflicted

Compassion is defined as "having deep sympathy or emotions for someone or something accompanied by the desire to help." When Jesus went about "doing good" in Acts 10:38, He was demonstrating the definition of compassion. We can see how "doing good" is related to "healing all who were oppressed of the devil" in the following two scriptures:

"... he that had been possessed with the devil prayed him that he might be with him. Howbeit Jesus suffered him not, but saith unto him, Go home to thy friends, and tell them how great things the Lord hath done for thee, and hath had compassion on thee" (Mark 5:18-19).

"And they brought him unto [Jesus]: and . . . straightway the spirit tare him; and he fell on the ground, and wallowed foaming. And he asked his father, How long is it ago since this came unto him? And he said, Of a child. And ofttimes it hath cast him into the fire, and into the waters, to destroy him: but if thou canst do any thing, have compassion on us, and help us. Jesus said unto him, If thou canst believe, all things are possible to him that believeth" (Mark 9:20-23).

3. Jesus Had Authority to Cast Out Demons

Whenever Jesus came into the presence of demons, they:

1) immediately recognized who Jesus was,

2) recognized that Jesus had authority over them, and

3) submitted to whatever Jesus commanded them to do.

This principle has great personal relevance for me. As I've shared earlier, when Jesus appeared to me to keep me from committing suicide, He allowed me to see the demons that had been assigned to me. The demons I saw reacted the same way the demons in the following scriptures did. They recognized and feared Jesus.

"And in the synagogue there was a man, which had a spirit of an unclean devil, and cried out with a loud voice, Saying, Let us alone; what have we to do with thee, thou Jesus of Nazareth? art thou come to destroy us?" (Luke 4:33-34).

"And cried with a loud voice, and said, What have I to do with thee, Jesus, thou Son of the most high God? I adjure thee by God, that thou torment me not" (Mark 5:7).

"... there met him two possessed with devils, . . . And, behold, they cried out, saying, What have we to do with thee, Jesus, thou Son of God? art thou come hither to torment us before the time?" (Matthew 8:28-29).

4. Jesus Used the Word of God to Combat the Devil

When Jesus dealt with devils, He did not negotiate with them. In His ministry, deliverance never took a long time. Jesus knew the authority He had over Satan and demons, and He thoroughly knew the Word of God. This was the basis of His success in overcoming the devil while on the earth.

Immediately after Jesus was baptized in the river Jordan, He was led into the wilderness where He was tempted by Satan. The devil first tempted Jesus with food. He said, *"If thou be the Son of God, command this stone that it be made bread"* (Luke 4:3). Jesus didn't argue or reason with Satan. He simply used the Word of God to combat the devil. *"And Jesus answered him, saying, It is written, That man shall not live by bread alone, but by every word of God"* (v. 4).

Satan next tempted Jesus with power. The devil told Jesus that he would give Him all the kingdoms of the world if He would bow down and worship him (vv. 5–7). Jesus again countered the devil's temptation with the Word of God. *"And Jesus answered and said unto him, Get thee behind me, Satan: for it is written, Thou shalt worship the Lord thy God, and him only shalt thou serve"* (v. 8).

Finally, Satan led Jesus to stand on the highest point of the temple in Jerusalem and taunted Jesus to jump off. Jesus continued to quote the Word: *"It is said, Thou shalt not tempt the Lord thy God. And when the devil had ended all the temptation, he departed from him for a season"* (v. 12).

The following verse shows that Jesus cast out spirits with His Word.

> *". . . they brought unto him many that were possessed with devils: and he cast out the spirits with his word, and healed all that were sick. . ."* (Matthew 8:16).

5. Immediate Deliverance From Devils

Casting a devil out of a person does not have to take a long period of time. And the person who needs deliverance is not permanently and negatively affected because of the demon possession. Every person that Jesus ministered to was immediately delivered and made whole.

Jesus prayed for a woman who had a spirit of infirmity that caused her to be bowed over for 18 years and *"... immediately she was made straight, and glorified God"* (Luke 13:13).

When the Syrophoenician woman begged Jesus to deliver her daughter, Scripture tells us that the child was *"... made whole from that very hour"* (Matt. 15:28). Although Jesus' disciples were unsuccessful in casting a devil out of a young boy, the spirit immediately came out upon Jesus command.

> *"... Thou dumb and deaf spirit, I charge thee, come out of him, and enter no more into him. And the spirit cried, and rent him sore, and came out of him..."* (Mark 9:25–26).

The Church's Assignment: Cast Out Devils

The Great Commission to the Church is found in Mark 16:15–18.

> *"... Go ye into all the world, and preach the gospel to every creature. He that believeth and is baptized shall be saved; but he that believeth not shall be damned"* (Mark 16:15–16).

Before Jesus ascended into heaven, He charged all Christians to go throughout the world and preach the Gospel. The book of Mark lists signs that will accompany Christians when they share the Good News of the Gospel. First on the list is casting out devils.

> *"And these signs shall follow them that believe; In my name shall they cast out devils..."* (Mark 16:17).

For the Church to successfully fulfill the Great Commission and complete its assignment from the Lord Jesus Christ, we—which includes all believers and not just full-time ministers—need to be involved in evangelism, healing, ministering the baptism of the Holy Spirit to people with the evidence of speaking in tongues, *and* casting out devils. Although I mentioned earlier, you can also see from the Great Commission that it would not be scriptural to have a ministry that focuses solely on deliverance or on baptizing people in the Holy Spirit, and so forth. God wants to bring wholeness to His people in proper balance.

That does not mean that we focus on the devil. Instead, we recognize that Satan is real and we need to deal with demons as a normal part of preaching the Gospel. I look at demons in the same way I look at paying my bills each month. While I don't really look forward to paying my utility bills, I'm not afraid of them. It's just part of life. This comparison might be unusual, but as you learn about and begin doing this component of ministry, you will eventually think, *Is this all there is to it?*

If you have ever hesitated or have been afraid of casting out demons, you will soon learn that you are not really doing anything. God is the one who is setting the person free. You just get the privilege of seeing another life made whole by your willingness to pray a very simple prayer of compassion for the person. Soon you will be wondering why you were ever afraid of casting out a demon. Eventually you will be saying, "Why did I ever wait so long to start!"

Chapter 13

A CHRISTIAN'S AUTHORITY

Satan thought he had conquered Jesus when the Son of God died on the Cross of Calvary. Little did Satan know that the Cross was *his* defeat. Jesus won a spiritual victory when He died on the Cross and rose from the dead. He defeated Satan once and for all and took back the keys of death, hell, and the grave (Col. 2:15, Rev. 1:18). And in defeating the devil, Jesus took back the dominion that Adam handed over to Satan during the fall of mankind in the Garden of Eden. Anyone who receives Jesus Christ as their Lord and Savior receives the same spiritual victory Christ won. We now have access to everything that belongs to Jesus because we have been blessed *". . . with all spiritual blessings in heavenly places in Christ"* (Eph. 1:3).

When Jesus ascended into heaven, He sat down at the right hand of the Father. Everything has been put under His feet, and His power, might, and dominion are above everything that is on the earth.

". . . when [God] raised [Christ] from the dead, and set him at his own right hand in the heavenly places, Far above all principality, and power, and might, and dominion, and every name that is named, not only in this world, but also in that which is to come: And hath put all things under his feet, and gave him to be the head over all things to the church" (Ephesians 1:20–22).

When you become born again, you are elevated to the same position that Christ is in.

"Even when we were dead in sins, hath quickened us together with Christ, . . . And hath raised us up together, and made us sit together in heavenly places in Christ Jesus" (Ephesians 2:5–6).

These scriptures show Jesus' victory over Satan.

> "And having spoiled principalities and powers, he made a shew of them openly, triumphing over them in it" (Colossians 2:15).
>
> "I am he that liveth, and was dead; and, behold, I am alive for evermore, Amen; and have the keys of hell and of death" (Revelation 1:18).

Our Authority Over Satan

When Adam fell through sin, all mankind lost their rightstanding with God and came under the dominion of Satan, the god of this world. In man's fallen state, Satan has authority over him. However, God made a way of escape for His beloved creation through the redemption that was purchased with the blood of Jesus Christ. If a person chooses redemption—or to be "saved"—the redeemed person rises above Satan's dominion. Satan and demons have not only lost their authority over born-again Christians, Christians now have authority over the devil!

While on the earth, Jesus gave His disciples authority over Satan. Today, this same authority has been given to all born-again Christians.

> "And when he had called unto him his twelve disciples, he gave them power against unclean spirits, to cast them out, and to heal all manner of sickness and all manner of disease" (Matthew 10:1).
>
> "Then he called his twelve disciples together, and gave them power and authority over all devils, and to cure diseases" (Luke 9:1).
>
> "And the seventy returned again with joy, saying, Lord, even the devils are subject unto us through thy name. And he said unto them, I beheld Satan as lightning fall from heaven. Behold, I give unto you power to tread on serpents and scorpions, and over all the power of the enemy: and nothing shall by any means hurt you" (Luke 10:17–19).

I learned from personal experience that you don't have to be a Bible scholar to walk in your authority in Christ. Even new Christians who don't yet have a firm grasp of the Word can use the name of Jesus to command devils to leave.

On the other hand, people who have not made Jesus the Lord and Savior of their lives do not have authority over Satan. The book of Acts records an incident where seven men tried to cast a demon out of an individual. These men, however, did not have a personal relationship with Jesus. They commanded the devils to leave by saying, *"We adjure you by Jesus whom Paul preacheth"* (Acts 19:13). Look what happened next!

> *"And the evil spirit answered and said, Jesus I know, and Paul I know; but who are ye? And the man in whom the evil spirit was leaped on them, and overcame them, and prevailed against them, so that they fled out of that house naked and wounded"* (Acts 19:15-16).

You can see that it is fruitless, as well as dangerous, to try and cast out demons when you don't have the authority to do so.

The following passage shows that only God's people can cast out devils. Until you make Jesus the Lord of your life, you are under the domain of Satan. And someone under the domain of Satan can't cast a demon out of another person under Satan's authority.

> *"And if Satan cast out Satan, he is divided against himself; how shall then his kingdom stand? And if I by Beelzebub cast out devils, by whom do your children cast them out?"* (Matthew 12:26-27).

When Jesus gave Christians the right to pray in His name, He gave them legal authority. A Christian using the name of Jesus is similar to the way a new wife begins to legally use her husband's surname. A new bride has the right to use her husband's name. She is entitled to write checks from a joint checking account. Merchants will accept checks from either the husband or the wife, because both names are on the account. In the same way, when believers use the name of Jesus to cast out devils, it is as though Jesus Himself were casting the devil out. In the spirit realm, there is no difference between Jesus casting out a devil or a believer casting out the devil.

These next scriptures show that Christians have a right to use the name of Jesus.

> *"And whatsoever ye shall ask in my name, that will I do, that the Father may be glorified in the Son. If ye shall ask any thing in my name, I will do it"* (John 14:13-14).

> *"And these signs shall follow them that believe; In my name shall they cast out devils. . ."* (Mark 16:17).

Freedom or Bondage: The Choice Is Yours

God desires for all people to be saved. First Timothy 2:3–4 says, *"For this is good and acceptable in the sight of God our Saviour; Who will have all men to be saved, and to come unto the knowledge of the truth."* The choice to follow God is up to you. He will never force His will on you. Matthew 7:13 (NIV) says, *"Enter through the narrow gate. For wide is the gate and broad is the road that leads to destruction, and many enter through it."* Unfortunately, many people will choose not to follow after God.

In the same way, God gives people the choice to be set free from the power of the devil. There are some cases where people do not want to give up the bondage they are in. And their will—their choice—can not be overridden. In cases like this, you should not pray for the person to be set free. The following passage of scripture shows what happens when demons are cast out of a person before the individual wants to be delivered.

> *"When the unclean spirit is gone out of a man, he walketh through dry places, seeking rest, and findeth none. Then he saith, I will return into my house from whence I came out; and when he is come, he findeth it empty, swept, and garnished. Then goeth he, and taketh with himself seven other spirits more wicked than himself, and they enter in and dwell there: and the last state of that man is worse than the first. . ."* (Matthew 12:43–45).

It can be heartbreaking when you want to help someone but they don't want your help. There is nothing you can do except pray for the person's heart to be opened to the good plan God has for them. But never underestimate the power of prayer. Although the person may not have been delivered and set free at that moment, the Lord will provide other opportunities. Just look at my life as an example. The Lord pursued me for years. When He finally got me, He turned me into an on-fire evangelist tirelessly pursuing lost people. Only God can reach a hard heart, but be encouraged because God *can* do it. It's His specialty!

Chapter 14

MY DELIVERANCE PROCESS

As I shared earlier, Jesus told me that I could be completely and instantly delivered. However, I couldn't see how that was possible because I was afraid. So Jesus led me through a deliverance process. As much as the Lord wanted me to be set free, He didn't want to frighten me by pushing deliverance on me. And as Christians ministering deliverance to people, we need to do the same. Eventually, I was completely set free.

The most important component of my deliverance process was learning the Word of God. It was through studying and meditating on the Word of God that gave me the solid foundation of the truth I needed. When I was involved in New Age, I studied all of the world's religions and became thoroughly confused as to what God was and was not. As Ephesians 5:26 states, I needed to be cleansed "... *with the washing of water by the word*" of all the religious errors that filled my mind. I have learned that the Word of God is the truth and our only safe harbor in life. As the scripture below states, the Word of God is the only thing that will set you free and keep you free:

> *"Then said Jesus . . . If ye continue in my word, . . . And ye shall know the truth, and the truth shall make you free"* (John 8:31–32).

When Jesus was tempted by the devil in the wilderness (Luke 4:1–11), He used the Word of God to overcome the devil. I learned that by following Jesus' example, I can also be victorious over the devil. The way I overcame the mental attacks of the devil was through learning and believing the truth of God's Word. It wasn't long before I overcame the battles in my mind. I then went on to receive victory in other areas like healing in my body, restored relationships, and so forth.

The Baptism in the Holy Spirit

Jesus did not leave you defenseless against Satan. Not only do you have the Word of God to stand on but you also have the Holy Spirit living inside of you. Here is what Jesus said about the Holy Spirit:

> "... the Comforter, which is the Holy Ghost, ... he shall teach you all things, and bring all things to your remembrance, whatsoever I have said unto you" (John 14:26).
> "... ye shall receive power, after that the Holy Ghost is come upon you: and ye shall be witnesses unto me ... unto the uttermost part of the earth" (Acts 1:8).

According to the Bible, the Baptism of the Holy Spirit is a separate experience that a believer can receive after salvation. The following scriptures describe the evidence of this baptism as the supernatural gift of speaking in other tongues.

> "And there appeared unto them cloven tongues like as of fire, and it sat upon each of them. And they were all filled with the Holy Ghost, and began to speak with other tongues, as the Spirit gave them utterance" (Acts 2:3–4).
> "And when Paul had laid his hands upon them, the Holy Ghost came on them; and they spake with tongues..." (Acts 19:6).

After I became born again, demons sometimes came back to test their limits. Because they once had a hold on me, they wanted to trick me into thinking they still had a hold on me. Some days I felt like I was a puppet, and whatever string Satan wanted to pull, is the experience I had. Fear, depression, discouragement, rejection. This is just what devils do, and it's very important to understand there is nothing wrong with you if you are experiencing this. But realize that you don't have to allow the devil to torment you any longer.

My freedom happened after I learned two truths: 1) my spiritual authority as a Christian and 2) the power of the baptism of the Holy Spirit. Through these spiritual weapons I learned how to say "No!" to the attacks of the enemy and how to cut those "puppet strings" for good.

My Deliverance Process

Here's what got me free and what keeps me free. My foundation is built on the Word of God. When combating tormenting thoughts, I first go to the Bible to find out what the Word has to say about my situation. Then when I pray, I include those scriptures in my prayer. However, I have learned that when I combine scripture with praying in the Spirit, my breakthrough comes faster.

I experienced some power when praying alone, but when I prayed with other sprit-filled Christians, the power behind our combined prayer was like nothing I had ever experienced before. I quickly learned that the devil doesn't stand a chance against a group of Christians praying together! After learning this, I joined several prayer groups in the church to learn from experienced prayer leaders how to pray with power and with balance.

The baptism in the Holy Spirit is a weapon God has given born-again believers to maintain the victory over the devil and his forces. When telling others why they need to receive the Holy Spirit in their lives, I like to use the following example. If soldiers are ordered to go to war but leave without their guns, their chances of survival are minimized. However, soldiers who have guns exponentially increase their chances of victory. To be a Christian without the baptism in the Holy Spirit is similar to being the soldier in a war without a gun.

Satan is in a battle for your soul. His primary goal is to keep you from becoming a Christian. And if you do become a Christian, he wants to trick you into not knowing the guaranteed victories you have now that you belong to God. Satan will do everything he can to cause you to live a defeated life. But why live that way anymore? As a Christian, essentially, you have made it. You are going to heaven and you can live a happy, power-packed life here before you go to heaven. Through the Word of God and the baptism in the Holy Spirit, you have everything you need to be victorious over the devil.

As a Christian, it would be tragic for you to have the tools that God worked so hard to get for you and then not use them. Your victorious life will actually cause more people to come to Christ because they will see you have the answer that they don't. You have learned the way out and what a joy it is to show others the way out as well.

Here are some scriptures that demonstrate the power of prayer:

> "How should one chase a thousand, and two put ten thousand to flight..." (Deuteronomy 32:30).

> "And if one prevail against him, two shall withstand him; and a threefold cord is not quickly broken" (Ecclesiastes 4:12).

> "... The effectual fervent prayer of a righteous man availeth much" (James 5:16).

> "But ye, beloved, building up yourselves on your most holy faith, praying in the Holy Ghost" (Jude 1:20).

STAYING FOCUSED ON GOD'S LOVE

One night, I was really struggling with condemnation over my past and insecurity and fear over my future. The devil was flooding me with thoughts that I had blown it too much for God to ever want me or use me. I didn't understand why I was being bombarded with these thoughts or being "attacked" by the devil when I was now a Christian. I have since learned that many of the great men and women of the Bible faced their greatest opposition when they were in the center of God's will. One look at the life of Apostle Paul proves this! When I was a young Christian and was experiencing an attack in my thought life, I often worked myself into a frenzy. I would quote scriptures, bind demons, and continuously repent until I wore wear myself out.

Eventually, I had to admit that this just wasn't working. The reason it didn't work for me was because I didn't understand how much God loved me. I was filled with so much condemnation, guilt, and insecurity that I couldn't understand why God would want me. Even though I was quoting scriptures to cast the devil out of my life, I really didn't think that I was worth God delivering. Because I still believed that, the devil took advantage of my feelings of inadequacy; and as a result, I stayed bound.

I came to realize that I was fighting the devil in the natural. Ephesians 6:12 says that our battle is not against flesh and blood, *"... but against principalities, against powers, against the rulers of the darkness of this*

My Deliverance Process

world, against spiritual wickedness in high places." And when thoughts come to your mind that are contrary to the Word of God, you must take these thoughts captive and force yourself to think in line with the Word (2 Cor. 10:5).

The Lord then led me to this scripture:

> *"There is no fear in love; but perfect love casteth out fear: because fear hath torment. . ."* (1 John 4:18).

I felt the Lord was telling me to quit working so hard to be set free. Instead, I just needed to simply receive His love. His direction to me felt like a drink of cool water on a hot muggy day. And I did it; I followed the Lord's advice. At first I felt irresponsible for not binding demons and repenting even though I no longer had anything to repent of. But my soul was at rest when I received God's love. After I received His love, I moved into faith and that ultimately brought peace.

I have built a solid foundation of God's Word in my heart and have developed a habit of praying in the Spirit. Now when a mental attack comes—meaning a flood of negative thoughts—I only have to quote a scripture and pray in the Spirit for a few minutes before getting a breakthrough. Before it took me weeks and sometimes months before I was set free. When I remain in the comfort and security of God's love, the devil's arrows bounce off of me. Jesus taught me how to allow His perfect love to cast out the fear and torment in my life, so I can walk in freedom.

I learned that a Christian's authority over demons and the ministry of deliverance is not focused on Satan. The power of your authority over demons is based in God's love. God loves you and doesn't want you to be tormented by the devil. It states in Isaiah 43:4 that you are precious to God and that He honors you. I can't think of anything more honoring than permanently driving out the dishonor and violation of demons in a person's life. God wants everyone to walk in victory over the devil.

The devil likes to work in extremes. His first goal is to keep you from ever repenting. Then if you do, he wants you to stay there and constantly repent for every little error you made. However, no one can live a whole, satisfied life if they are always thinking there is something wrong with them. If the devil can trick you into believing you are flawed, you can never rise up and stand in your spiritual wholeness as a Christian. He knows if you don't know how to stand in your wholeness, he can not only wreak havoc in your life, but you will also never have confidence in God to set others free from the devil's grip.

Someone once told me a story of how to stop fighting if you are in a tug of war. All you need to do is drop your end of the rope and walk away. That's it! And that's how it is with the devil. If you are a Christian, the fight is over. Jesus won. Satan lost. So drop the rope and walk away. Rest in Jesus' love. That is victory. And that is the limit of how much we should "fight" the devil. In essence, you don't. We don't have to buy into the illusion that there even is a fight. Just stand in your authority under a loving God's protection, walk in freedom, and set others free, in Jesus' name!

Chapter 15

SETTING PEOPLE FREE

I have been grateful to have many opportunities to set people free, or minister deliverance, to others by using the simple, biblical principles I have learned. Nothing shows that you are free more than being able to minister freedom and victory to someone else! The ultimate payback for all the pain Satan caused me throughout my life is winning souls and setting as many people free as possible. First John 5:4 states, ". . . *this is the victory that overcomes the world [Satan], even our faith.*" Rather than feeling intimidated with the deliverance component of ministry, I feel more like Indiana Jones. I'm going straight into enemy forces and recapturing stolen treasure. And the lost treasure is people! I am thrilled over every person who is saved and made whole.

The Lord has empowered me through the Word of God and walking in the power of the Holy Spirit to turn the tables on the devil and set others free from the same bondages I had been trapped in. All Christians have been given the exact same power and authority. I know it brings God great joy when we know the spiritual authority we have as Christians and have the courage to walk it out. I encourage you to thoroughly enjoy your dominion over Satan; I do! It's my payback. And it's your payback too!

If we don't step up and do this for others, who will? Just as the Lord showed me in the vision of the lost (see graphic: The Lost), He told me no one was going to help them because so many Christians don't want to be bothered. In the same way that Jesus asked me, "Would you help them as I helped you?", I encourage you to answer the same call that I did. Would you help others as Christ has helped you?

Your Authority Over Devils

When I began ministering to others, I studied scriptures that were full of God's power. Then I personalized them. Here's an example:

> *"And the evil spirit answered and said, Jesus I know, and Paul I know. . ."* (Acts 19:15).

I personalized this scripture by declaring out loud: "Jesus I know, Paul I know, and Lori I know!"

I also adapted Luke 10:17–19 as follows, and declared it out loud until I believed it:

> *". . . even the devils are subject unto (Lori) through thy name. And he said unto (Lori), I beheld Satan as lightning fall from heaven. Behold, I give unto (Lori) power to tread on serpents and scorpions, and over all the power of the enemy: and nothing shall by any means hurt (Lori)."*

I encourage you to find scriptures that speak to your heart and do the same until you are filled with bold confidence. Soon, you will not be intimidated by the devil. I'm not anymore, and you shouldn't be either!

Soul Winning for Christ

After my salvation, I immediately began winning souls to Christ. Right from the start, Jesus was very clear about what my assignment was. Although I didn't really know what I was doing, I just started and learned along the way. I thought if Jesus could rescue me moments before I was going to commit suicide, He could certainly correct me if I witnessed to people incorrectly. If He didn't correct me, I thought I must be doing okay. I think many Christians are so afraid that they will do something wrong that they never get started in soul winning.

What's the worst that can happen? If you witness to somebody and they don't get saved, that's the worst thing that could happen. You've done your part, and God will back you. He always does when your motives are pure. When I started witnessing to people, sometimes I would tell a portion of my testimony. At other times, I would share the few scriptures I knew that told people how to be saved. Please refer to the following page for a sample soul winning prayer. This approach focuses on God's love, as Romans 2:4 (NIV) states, *"God's kindness leads (people) toward repentance."* Now when I go out witnessing I just follow my heart as I speak to people.

Witnessing to others is preaching the Gospel, and casting out devils is part of preaching the Gospel. I often came across people who needed deliverance. And probably because I didn't know any better, I did for them what Jesus did for me. I commanded demons to leave in Jesus' name. Many people need to be set free from the power of the devil, and the Church is the only force that can help these people. But know that when you cast them out, they have to go. You can do it!

Almost all of the experiences I've had in ministering deliverance to others happened while I was out in the general public. This is how it happened in Jesus' ministry as well. He went to the people who needed Him, and we need to do the same. There are so many people who need God's love, healing, and deliverance. Opportunities to help people are always available. But it's up to Christians to go into the world and minister the Good News.

I quickly joined the street evangelism team in my church where I was properly trained me on how to win souls and how to walk in God's healing and delivering power. I volunteered in that area for seven years. I now go to churches and train people on how to develop their own street evangelism outreach. You can also witness on your own, and I make myself available anytime God wants me to help someone. However, there is a greater power and safety when you witness with others. And it's just more fun too! I encourage you to join up with other Christians and start your own outreach at your church if it already doesn't have a street evangelism outreach.

The Church is still in the book of Acts, and should be walking in the same power now that Jesus' disciples did then. Signs and wonders should follow you today. It's a natural fruit of preaching the Gospel. Soul winning and street evangelism is walking in the book of Acts in your own backyard.

Soul Winning Prayer

Witnessing is best with groups of 2-3 people, including at least one male and one female in each group.

—Approach—

Hello. I just wanted to tell you that God loves you and that He has a good plan for your life. I'm sure you already know that.

Can I ask you a question? If something happened to you today, do you know if you would go to heaven? Most people hope or think that they will go to heaven, but they aren't sure. Or, they just don't want to think about it.

The Bible says that every one of us will live forever, either with God or apart from God. He loves us so much that He leaves the choice up to us. God sent Jesus here for you to bring you back home to God, but the choice is up to you.

The Bible says that we've each done wrong and that we have to tell God we're sorry and mean it. After we've done that, God will restore us. Anyone who calls on Jesus will be saved and be able to spend eternity in heaven.

—Pray—

I'd like to say a quick prayer for you. (I have the most success when I just start praying for them. Prayer softens the person's heart to receive more.)

God, you created ____Name_____ to live as your son/daughter. God, You've been speaking to them throughout their entire lives. I ask that you speak deep in their heart right now and tell them how much You love them.

(Continue praying for the person and believe God for specific words to comfort them. Believe God to heal or deliver the person if needed. It is at this point in the prayer when I see most miracles happen. After receiving a healing or deliverance, many people will quickly receive salvation.)

_____Name_____ if there are areas in your heart and life you know you are holding back from God, I pray that right now, you choose to give those areas to God. Let's pray for you give your life to God and be saved.

Dear Lord Jesus, I give you my whole self right now. I let go of my old life and choose to live for God. Forgive me for doing wrong. I am sorry. God, save me and make me into the person you want me to be. In Jesus' name. Amen.

(If possible, continue praying with the person for the Baptism of the Holy Spirit.)

—Follow-up—

Congratulations! Now that you are saved, God wants to help you in every area of your life. I'd like to help you with a couple of things, like reading the Bible and learning how to pray. Could I call you this week to check on you? What's your #? (Men should only ask men for contact information and women should only ask women.)

Do you have a church you go to? Which one?

(If no church) I belong to a great church, and I'd like to invite you to come with my family.

Setting People Free

First Corinthians 15:57 says, *"...thanks be to God, which giveth us the victory through our Lord Jesus Christ."* Here are some testimonies that I've personally seen of God setting people free from the power of the devil just because I was willing and available for what God needed.

Deliverance of a Gang Member

I was running errands on my way home from work. I saw that I needed gas so I pulled into a gas station to fill up my car. As I was pumping gas, I noticed two young men in the parking lot. The Lord prompted me to witness to them. I keep Gospel tracts in my purse and car. I always like to have them on hand.

After I filled my car with gas, I walked over to the young men with tracts for each of them. They were both dressed in black and you could tell they dyed their hair very dark. One of the young men a lot of tattoos, piercings, and chains. The other looked a little more average, but he was very dirty. It looked as though he had been in some trouble or spent a couple of nights on the streets.

I began by telling them that I felt the Lord wanted me to let them know that He loved them and that He had a good plan for their lives. They responded by telling me a little of their stories. Earlier that day, they had been shot at while in their home. They then came to the gas station to figure out what to do next. We talked for a short while, and they shared that they were both gang members and were constantly in fear for their lives.

I told them that heaven and hell are real places and that God spared them from going to hell just hours earlier that day. I shared some of my testimony. And after talking some more, they said they would like to receive Christ. However, as soon as they agreed to pray the sinner's prayer, the gang member with the tattoos began manifesting a demon. His face and eyes changed in front of me. I watched as darkness that was not human flickered back and forth in his eyes. He then pulled a knife on me and started smiling. The demon was testing me. The young man kept moving the knife back and forth in front of me to intimidate me.

Before I had time to think, the power of God rose up in me, and I said in a loud, authoritative voice, "Put that knife away and repeat after me." His hand that was holding the knife sort of crumpled, and he calmly put the knife away and bowed his head. I was so shocked that I forgot to start praying. The young man looked up at me when I didn't say anything. I could tell he was in his right mind. I don't think the young man was even aware of what the demon had just done through him. I shook my head, and said, "Oh." Then I led him in a prayer and he got saved. The other gang member stepped away when his friend pulled the knife on me. When he saw his friend praying, he was shocked and came back over. You could see the fear of God in His eyes. He knew that God had done something supernatural. He bowed his head in prayer and got saved too!

Deliverance of Two Homosexual Men

Another time, when I was part of a street evangelism team, we were witnessing in a bar district late at night. One of these bars happened to be a gay bar. I love witnessing to people caught up in homosexual lifestyles. I find that they have a similar deception to what I experienced in New Age, so I can relate to where they are coming from.

My teammate and I met two men who were about to go into the gay bar. We began telling them how much Jesus loved them. As we talked, I assumed they were trying to figure out a way to get away from us as quickly as possible. I was sure wrong! They intently listened to everything we said. Please never judge anyone. Everyone deserves the miracles and love of God equally. You don't know the hurts anyone has gone through that led them into a particular sin or lifestyle.

The men shared how they both tried to go to church but were asked to leave. They said both of their families were Christian, but they were embarrassed of them and didn't want them in their church. My heart broke as the two shared their stories of rejection. They told us they didn't want to be gay, but they didn't know how to get out of this lifestyle.

My teammate and I told them that both angels and demons are real. We explained how demons can influence people's behavior and trap them in sin. I shared part of my testimony to hopefully make them feel that we weren't judging them but that we truly wanted to help them. (Please note: Not everyone in an alternative lifestyle is oppressed or possessed. In this case, the two men happened to be.) They both agreed to receive Christ as their Savior.

We started praying and told the men to repeat, "Dear Lord Jesus. . . ." One of the men could not say Jesus' name. We repeated that portion of the prayer. I watched as the man tried to say Jesus' name. He bent forward and began throwing up. When he stood up, his countenance was changed. He even started smiling. We celebrated with them and explained what had just happened to them. We finished leading him and his partner in a prayer of salvation. This time he was able to say the name of Jesus. They were so happy to be Christians, as well as to finally be accepted by some Christians.

Deliverance of a Former Satanist

Another great deliverance happened while I was training another church how to do soul winning. While on the streets, I met a young man who was selling flowers. He was very pleasant to our team but was obviously troubled in his emotions. As he shared his story, we learned that he had formerly been involved in Satan worship of some kind and didn't think God would take him back because of what he had done. Compassion for him rose up inside of me. I knew how the devil condemned me about my past. Even after I shared my past, he was still very closed and ashamed of what he'd done. He eventually shared that he had made animal sacrifices to Satan and believed God wouldn't take him back. I felt bad for him as I thought of the torment he must be experiencing.

I hugged him and shared scriptures with him about God's love. I shared more of my own testimony and how God took me back. He listened as I shared things about myself that I wasn't particularly excited to share. But I had to push my dignity out of the way for the compassion I felt for his soul. I once heard a minister say, "Don't waste your wasted years. Someone needs to hear it to be set free."

After I shared my story, the young man eventually let us pray for him. As I prayed, my own deliverance flashed through my mind. I remembered how Jesus told me I could have received immediate and total deliverance, but I was not able to receive it. I knew when I prayed that this man would receive his deliverance through a process as well. So I didn't tell the devil to go. Instead, I did exactly what Jesus did for me. I simply shared the message of God's love to him and told him that God accepted him exactly the way he was. I felt it was better to lead him to Jesus rather than trying to drive the devil from him before he was ready. This man rededicated his life to Christ. I believe that he received a partial deliverance that night. I saw this man the next night by coincidence. His entire countenance changed. As we talked, he looked me straight in the face. The night before, he couldn't do that. He always looked away in shame.

The above stories are only three examples of deliverances that I have been privileged to help people with. If I can do this coming out of the spiritual bondages I was in, *anyone* can share Christ and set people free. The need for Christians to be strong and full of the power of God and yet balanced with the love and compassion of Jesus is great. The world doesn't have answers; the world has the needs. Jesus gave the Church the answers, and you and I must help those who have nowhere else to go to get freedom. Jesus gave the Church the supernatural power to thrive. As people see wholeness, victory, and power in your life, they will be drawn to you. And I encourage you to be the answer to someone else's freedom.

Hell

Chapter 16

HELL IS REAL

> "And on some have compassion, . . . but others save with fear, pulling them out of the fire. . . ."
>
> —Jude 1:22–23 (NKJV)

Hell is a very real place. At the time of my conversion, I didn't believe in hell. However, just because I didn't believe hell was real didn't change the fact that I would have gone there if I had died as an unsaved person. I had no idea when Jesus intervened before my suicide attempt at how close I was to spending an eternity in hell. I had no idea how close to hell I was the night I refused to respond to the altar call to repent. But after I stared into a very real hell, desperate and humbled, the Lord ultimately saved me with fear "*. . . pulling me out of the fire.*"

Colossians 1:27–28 states "*. . . Christ in you, the hope of glory, Whom we preach, warning every man. . . .*" From these verses, we see that the love and hope of Jesus cannot be preached without also warning people about the consequence of rejecting Him. And the consequence is an eternal life in hell.

As I openly shared throughout this book, even though I had spiritual experiences where I saw Jesus, that is not what saved me. What saved me from hell was believing that Jesus died on the Cross to pay the penalty for the sin of mankind *and* repenting of my sins. This chapter is filled with many scriptures that describe hell, and my prayer is that if you have not yet surrendered your life to the Lord, you would do so immediately. Then, please warn everyone you know about this real place, so no one within your influence will ever have to go to hell.

Hell is an Actual Place

The Bible makes many references to hell as an actual place:

> "For a fire is kindled in mine anger, and shall burn unto the lowest hell, . . . They shall be burnt with hunger, and devoured with burning heat, and with bitter destruction. . ." (Deuteronomy 32:22, 24).
>
> "Let death seize upon them, and let them go down quick into hell. . ." (Psalm 55:15).
>
> "Hell is naked before him. . ." (Job 26:6).
>
> "Her house is the way to hell, going down to the chambers of death" (Proverbs 7:27).
>
> "Hell and destruction are never full; so the eyes of man are never satisfied" (Proverbs 27:20).
>
> "Hell from beneath is moved for thee to meet thee at thy coming: it stirreth up the dead for thee. . ." (Isaiah 14:9).
>
> "Yet thou shalt be brought down to hell, to the sides of the pit" (Isaiah 14:15).
>
> "I made the nations to shake at the sound of his fall, when I cast him down to hell with them that descend into the pit. . ." (Ezekiel 31:16).
>
> "And fear not them which kill the body, but are not able to kill the soul: but rather fear him which is able to destroy both soul and body in hell" (Matthew 10:28).
>
> "And I say also unto thee, That thou art Peter, and upon this rock I will build my church; and the gates of hell shall not prevail against it" (Matthew 16:18).

Two Sections of Hell

Most people use the term "hell" in a general sense. But the Bible actually uses several terms to define the different areas of hell. A lot of people use these words interchangeably because they don't understand the meaning behind each term. Each area of hell was assigned a specific purpose. These terms used to describe hell are sheol, hades, gehenna, and the lake of fire.

In the Hebrew, *sheol* refers to the spiritual location of the dead. It literally means "the place of the dead" or the "place of departed spirits."

I believe this is what I saw when I described my torture cell. I knew that what I was seeing was only a holding place and I would be sent to another place in hell later. In the Greek, *hades* is the word that refers to hell, specifically the temporary location of the dead.

After Christ's resurrection, *sheol* and *hades* now describe the same place. However, prior to Jesus' work of redemption, *sheol* had two compartments as seen in the following verses:

> *"And it came to pass, that the beggar died, and was carried by the angels into Abraham's bosom: the rich man also died, and was buried; And in hell he lift up his eyes, being in torments, and seeth Abraham afar off, and Lazarus in his bosom. And he cried and said, Father Abraham, have mercy on me, and send Lazarus, that he may dip the tip of his finger in water, and cool my tongue; for I am tormented in this flame"* (Luke 16:22–24).

Prior to the resurrection of Christ, one of the compartments in *sheol* was Abraham's bosom, which the Bible also referred to as paradise. It was a holding place for the righteous who would later join Jesus in heaven. In the next scripture David says that his soul will not remain in *sheol*.

> *"For thou wilt not leave my soul in hell* [sheol]*; neither wilt thou suffer thine Holy One to see corruption"* (Psalm 16:10).

Ephesians 4:8 describes what happened in *sheol* at the time of Christ's resurrection: *"Wherefore he saith, When he ascended up on high, he led captivity captive, and gave gifts unto men."* Jesus led the righteous out of *sheol* and carried those souls into heaven. Now all righteous people— or people who have been born again—no longer wait in *sheol*. They are immediately brought to the Lord's presence. When Jesus talked to the thief on the cross, He said, *". . . Today shalt thou be with me in paradise"* (Luke 23:42–43).

The other side of *sheol* serves as a holding place for the wicked. This is true for the wicked who died both before and after the resurrection of Jesus. This is where the rich man in Luke 16 was held. The terms *sheol* and *hades* can be used interchangeably to refer to the present holding place of lost souls. If I had not become born again and died in that state, this is the place in hell where I would be right now.

We see from the following scriptures that the exact location of *sheol* or *hades* is in the center of the earth:

> *"And the earth opened her mouth, and swallowed them up, . . . They, and all that appertained to them, went down alive into the pit, and the earth closed upon them. . ."* (Numbers 16:32–33).
>
> *". . . for they are all delivered unto death, to the nether parts of the earth, in the midst of the children of men, with them that go down to the pit"* (Ezekiel 31:14).
>
> *"Now that he ascended, what is it but that he also descended first into the lower parts of the earth?"* (Ephesians 4:9).
>
> *"But those that seek my soul, to destroy it, shall go into the lower parts of the earth"* (Psalm 63:9).

The terms *gehenna* and the lake of fire are used in reference to hell. *Gehenna* is a Greek word that refers to the lake of fire.

> *"But I say unto you, . . . whosoever shall say, Thou fool, shall be in danger of hell [gehenna] fire"* (Matthew 5:22).

THE LAKE OF FIRE

The lake of fire refers to the final judgment of God for Satan, demons, and those who have rejected Jesus. At the coming great white throne judgment, *sheol*, or *hades*, will be delivered into the lake of fire or *gehenna*. When I saw into hell, I knew that as bad as this section was, something far worse was coming. And that was the lake of fire.

> *"The Lord knoweth how to deliver the godly out of temptations, and to reserve the unjust unto the day of judgment to be punished"* (2 Peter 2:9).
>
> *"But the heavens and the earth, which are now, by the same word are kept in store, reserved unto fire against the day of judgment and perdition of ungodly men"* (2 Peter 3:7).

> "And the beast was taken, and with him the false prophet that wrought miracles before him, with which he deceived them that had received the mark of the beast, and them that worshipped his image. These both were cast alive into a lake of fire burning with brimstone" (Revelation 19:20).

> "And the devil that deceived them was cast into the lake of fire and brimstone, . . . and shall be tormented day and night for ever and ever. And I saw a great white throne, and him that sat on it, . . . And I saw the dead, small and great, stand before God; and the books were opened: and another book was opened, which is the book of life: and the dead were judged out of those things which were written in the books, according to their works. And the sea gave up the dead which were in it; and death and hell delivered up the dead which were in them: and they were judged every man according to their works. And death and hell were cast into the lake of fire. This is the second death. And whosoever was not found written in the book of life was cast into the lake of fire" (Revelation 20:10-15).

> "Then shall he say also unto them on the left hand, Depart from me, ye cursed, into everlasting fire, prepared for the devil and his angels" (Matthew 25:41).

HEAVEN

The Bible is very clear about where born again Christians go when they die:

> ". . . to be absent from the body, and to be present with the Lord" (2 Corinthians 5:8).

The Apostle Paul struggled with staying on earth or dying, which he equated to immediately being with the Lord in heaven:

> "For I am in a strait betwixt two, having a desire to depart, and to be with Christ; which is far better: Nevertheless to abide in the flesh is more needful for you" (Philippians 1:23-24).

For the Christian, there is no fear of death. Because of the death, burial, and resurrection of Jesus, death no longer has a sting and is swallowed up in victory (1 Cor. 15:56-57). All Christians will spend an eternity in heaven. But for those who haven't accepted Jesus as their Lord and Savior and refuse to repent of their sin, there is much to fear.

Chapter 17

LIFE IN HELL

When unsaved people descend into hell, their senses remain intact. Although they do not have a physical body, they are still able to smell, see, and hear. They will experience thirst and still have physical senses and emotions. The following scriptures support this:

> "Let death take my enemies by surprise; let them go down alive to the grave. . ." (Psalm 55:15 NIV).

> ". . . it is profitable for thee that one of thy members should perish, and not that thy whole body should be cast into hell" (Matthew 5:29–30).

> "And in hell he lift up his eyes, being in torments, and seeth Abraham afar off, and Lazarus in his bosom. And he cried and said, Father Abraham, have mercy on me, and send Lazarus, that he may dip the tip of his finger in water, and cool my tongue; for I am tormented in this flame" (Luke 16:23–24).

Intense physical and emotional sorrow will be experienced in hell, as described in the passages below:

> "And shall cast them into a furnace of fire: there shall be wailing and gnashing of teeth" (Matthew 13:42).
>
> "The sorrows of death compassed me, and the pains of hell got hold upon me: I found trouble and sorrow" (Psalm 116:3).

The physical body of a person in hell still requires sleep and rest, yet that person will never again be able to sleep.

> ". . . and he shall be tormented with fire and brimstone in the presence of the holy angels, and in the presence of the Lamb: And

the smoke of their torment ascendeth up for ever and ever: and they have no rest day nor night..." (Revelation 14:10-11).

DEMONS

Demons are able to torment people in hell. The Bible even describes the kinds of torment and the degrees of torment that will be experienced. From what I saw in the few moments I looked into hell, I know if I had experienced similar torture on earth, it would have quickly killed me. Although my torture would have been more severe because I had been a false prophet, every part of hell, for each soul in hell, is utter torment as these scriptures indicate:

"I will heap mischiefs upon them; I will spend mine arrows upon them. They shall be burnt with hunger, and devoured with burning heat, and with bitter destruction: I will also send the teeth of beasts upon them, with the poison of serpents of the dust. The sword without, and terror within, shall destroy..." (Deuteronomy 32:23-24).

"... he shall be brought to the king of terrors [death]" (Job 18:14 AMP).

"Yes, his soul draws near to corruption, and his life to the inflicters of death (the destroyers)" (Job 33:22 AMP).

"And his lord was wroth, and delivered him to the tormentors..." (Matthew 18:34).

CHAINS AND PRISON CELLS

As I describe earlier, I literally saw the prison cell that Satan had prepared for me. The Bible also describes prison cells and chained restraints for the occupants of hell.

"Her house is the way to hell, going down to the chambers of death" (Proverbs 7:27).

"And they will be gathered together as prisoners are gathered in a pit or dungeon; they will be shut up in prison..." (Isaiah 24:22 AMP).

"For if God spared not the angels that sinned, but cast them down to hell, and delivered them into chains of darkness, to be reserved unto judgment" (2 Peter 2:4).

"And the angels which kept not their first estate, but left their own habitation, he hath reserved in everlasting chains under darkness unto the judgment of the great day" (Jude 1:6).

Fire

Many scriptures in the Bible describe fire when referring to hell. From my experience, I saw a gust of fire in hell ready to consume my prison cell. Some scriptures also indicate pits of fire and burning. Other verses talk about the torment that will be experienced in the lake of fire. Following are some of these references:

"Let burning coals fall upon them: let them be cast into the fire; into deep pits. . ." (Psalm 140:10).

"And shall cast them into the furnace of fire: there shall be wailing and gnashing of teeth" (Matthew 13:50).

". . . it is better for thee to enter into life maimed, than having two hands to go into hell, into the fire that never shall be quenched" (Mark 9:43).

"Even as Sodom and Gomorrha, and the cities about them in like manner, . . . are set forth for an example, suffering the vengeance of eternal fire" (Jude 1:7).

"And death and hell were cast into the lake of fire. This is the second death" (Revelation 20:14).

Lost Forever

One of the most painful aspects of hell is eternal separation from God. When the devil tried to take me to hell, I saw that I was leaving all light and life. I knew that if I went to hell, I would never again experience love or hope. Seeing the absolutes of the different realms was shocking and terrifying to me. I saw what life and death looked like in the spirit realm. For a moment, I saw and felt what it would be like to spend an eternity without the Lord, and it changed me forever. The scriptures below point out eternal separation from God:

> "From the wicked their light is withheld, and their uplifted arm is broken. Have the gates of death been revealed to you? Or have you seen the doors of deep darkness? Where is the way where light dwells? And as for darkness, where is its abode" (Job 38:15, 17, 19 AMP).

> "For the grave cannot praise thee, death can not celebrate thee: they that go down into the pit cannot hope for thy truth" (Isaiah 38:18).

> ". . . strangers from the covenants of promise, having no hope, and without God. . ." (Ephesians 2:12).

> "Who shall be punished with everlasting destruction from the presence of the Lord, and from the glory of his power. . ." (2 Thessalonians 1:9).

Who Goes to Hell and Who Goes to Heaven

Hell was never intended for mankind, but the Bible is very clear on who will go there. I understood during my experience of hell that it was my willingness to repent of sin and believe in Jesus that saved me from eternity in hell. The following scriptures deifne who will go to hell:

> "I tell you, Nay: but, except ye repent, ye shall all likewise perish" (Luke 13:3).

> "In flaming fire taking vengeance on them that know not God, and that obey not the gospel of our Lord Jesus Christ" (2 Thessalonians 1:8).

> "But the fearful, and unbelieving, and the abominable, and murderers, and whoremongers, and sorcerers, and idolaters, and all liars, shall have their part in the lake which burneth with fire and brimstone: which is the second death" (Revelation 21:8).

The Bible is also very clear on who will go to heaven and how you can be confident that you will go there when you die. God has written the requirements so simply that even a child can understand them. The following scriptures show who will go to heaven:

> "For God so loved the world, that he gave his only begotten Son, that whosoever believeth in him should not perish, but have everlasting life.

For God sent not his Son into the world to condemn the world; but that the world through him might be saved" (John 3:16–17).

"Much more then, being now justified by his blood, we shall be saved from wrath through him" (Romans 5:9).

"And to wait for his Son from heaven, whom he raised from the dead, even Jesus, which delivered us from the wrath to come" (1 Thessalonians 1:10).

People sometimes joke about going to hell, but they really have no idea what they are saying. No one should go to this place. God never meant for any person to go there. I trust that my sharing a glimpse of the horrors of hell will cause you to make drastic changes in your life if you are on that broad road to death.

Chapter 18

ARE YOU SAVED?

God loves you and has provided a way of escape from the torments of hell. Since the fall of Adam in the Garden of Eden, mankind has been separated from God. Romans 3:23 says that *". . . all have sinned, and come short of the glory of God."* In and of yourself, you can't do anything to earn your way into heaven and back into God's presence. It doesn't matter how good you are or what good you have done for your fellow man, no amount of good deeds will gain your entrance into heaven.

However, God loves you so much that He sent His Son Jesus Christ to make a way for you and all of mankind to be brought back into His presence. It's only through Jesus Christ that you receive forgiveness of sin and can spend an eternity in heaven when you die. Romans 6:23 says, *"For the wages of sin is death, but the gift of God is eternal life in Christ Jesus our Lord."* Ephesians 2:8–9 says that it is by *". . . grace that you have been saved through faith, and that not of yourself; it is the gift of God, not of works lest anyone should boast."*

God did not send His son into the world to condemn you. On the contrary, it's through Jesus Christ and Him alone that you can be saved (John 3:17). It says in John 3:36, *"He that believeth on the Son hath everlasting life: and he that believeth not the Son shall not see life. . . ."*

Recognizing and repenting of your sinful state and believing that Jesus died on the Cross to save you from your sins is the *only* way to heaven. It's really that simple. It's a one-time decision and event that will change your life. But the choice is up to you. God will never force you to follow after Him. My prayer is that you will choose to follow after Jesus today.

My life is an example of what it was like to follow my own plan. And my experience of seeing hell gives you a glimpse of what is in store for those who reject God. You don't have to experience what I went through. You can receive God's forgiveness of sin by trusting in Jesus Christ. John 1:12 says, *"But as many as received Him, to them He gave the right to become the children of God, to those who believe in His name."*

You can't imagine what God can do with your life when you surrender it to Him. I could have never imagined all of the good things God had in store for me by surrendering my life to him. Your transformation may or may not be as extreme as mine. But if God could transform my life, just think what He could do in yours. Don't let one more day go by without belonging to God. Just as He pursued me with His love and mercy, He is pursuing you. And in the same way He stretched out His hand to me, asking me to say "yes" to Him, He is asking you to say "yes" to Him.

Receive God's forgiveness and His gift of eternal life right now. Pray this prayer:

> *Dear Heavenly Father:*
>
> *I admit that I am a sinner, and I repent of my sins. I acknowledge my need of a Savior. I believe that you sent your Son, Jesus Christ, to the earth to pay the penalty for sin. I believe that Jesus died on the Cross and rose from the dead. And I receive the gift of eternal life that you have provided through Him. I thank you for forgiving me. I thank you for saving me and showing me the good plan you have for my life.*
>
> *In Jesus' name. Amen.*

You have just made the best decision of your life. You now are a child of God. To begin growing with the Lord, you need to attend a good Bible believing church that believes in being born again. I encourage you to attend regularly so you are taught the Word of God. If you don't already have a Bible, get one, and read it every day. A good place to start is the book of John. Then read through the New Testament and let God start speaking to you from the scriptures. Ask Him to connect

Are You Saved?

you with some good Christian friends to help you grow in your new life. Make time to pray every day. And remember that prayer is really just having a conversation with God.

The other free gift that God has promised is the baptism of the Holy Spirit with the evidence of speaking in other tongues. This gift is available to all Christians, and by receiving it, God grants the supernatural power needed to have a victorious Christian life.

Acts 19:2 states, *". . . Have ye received the Holy Ghost since ye believed?"* This shows that the Holy Spirit is a gift for you to receive after salvation.

Receive the baptism of the Holy Spirit. Pray this prayer:

Dear Heavenly Father,

In the same way that I received salvation as a free gift from you, I now receive the baptism of the Holy Spirit and the ability to pray in other tongues. Thank you Lord.

In Jesus' name. Amen.

To learn more about the baptism of the Holy Spirit, contact your pastor at your local church and join a Spirit-filled prayer group to learn how to pray.

*For God so loved the world that
He gave His only begotten Son,
that whoever believes in Him should
not perish but have everlasting life.*

*For God did not send His Son into the
world to condemn the world, but
that the world through Him might be saved.*

—John 3:16–17

Lori Haider Ministries

Saving Souls • Training Soul Winners

For more information contact:

P.O. Box 46194

Plymouth, MN 55446

www.savedfromhell.org

www.ingramcontent.com/pod-product-compliance
Lightning Source LLC
Chambersburg PA
CBHW071929290426
44110CB00013B/1532